# Western Rider's Handbook

Also by Karen W. Carden:

The Persecuted Prophets (with Robert W. Pelton)

# WESTERN RIDER'S HANDBOOK

Karen W. Carden

SOUTH BRUNSWICK AND NEW YORK: A. S. BARNES AND COMPANY
LONDON: THOMAS YOSELOFF LTD

© 1976 by A. S. Barnes and Co., Inc.

A. S. Barnes and Co., Inc.
Cranbury, New Jersey 08512

Thomas Yoseloff Ltd
108 New Bond Street
London W1Y OQX, England

**Library of Congress Cataloging in Publication Data**

Carden, Karen W
  Western rider's handbook.

  Includes index.
  1. Horses—The West. 2. Horsemanship. 3. Show
riding—The West. I. Title.
SF284.U5C37    1975    636.1'00978    75-5171
ISBN 0-498-01631-5

**To
my mother, my father, and Ray,
all of whom have alternately
nurtured and endured my obsession with horses**

# Contents

# Preface

Western riding is an enjoyable part of the horse world that is uniquely American. The traditions are our own, born on the Western frontier and largely unchanged, even today. The cowboy hats with their tightly rolled brims, the big, deep-seated saddles, and trim leather chaps bring the romance of yesterday's Old West onto the trails and into the show rings of the twentieth century.

This functional as well as colorful mode of riding is rapidly growing in popularity with the exhibitor, the pleasure rider and the spectator. This book was written in response to that trend. It is for the average knowledgeable horseman. It is not designed to teach horse maintenance or riding skills. Neither does it include advanced training procedures or highly specialized techniques. It is written solely to acquaint the reader with the way things are done, Western style.

Do you know what bandanas were used for besides robbing banks? What is a pigging string? What do judges look for in a stock seat equitation class? WESTERN RIDER'S HANDBOOK is exactly that — a handbook. It describes what is required to be a well-dressed Westerner. It offers basic show rules of the leading Western horse associations. It contains how-to tips used by some of the nation's top trainers.

This handy reference book is a collection of factual information, without being a volume of facts. If it does not have an answer you are looking for, it will tell you where or how to find it. The author does not rely only on her personal knowledge, but has thoroughly researched

Western riding from Tennessee to Texas and from Kentucky to
California.

# Acknowledgments

I would like to express my deep gratitude to Robert W. Pelton for his extensive role in the creation and emergence of this book.

Appreciation goes to the following contributors for their prompt, enthusiastic participation in my research: *Appaloosa News*; the American Morgan Horse Association, Inc.; the American Quarter Horse Association; Mr. Joe Brownlee, owner, and Mr. Earl Burchett, trainer, Hidden Hills Farms; International Arabian Horse Association; The Tony Lama Company, Inc.; The H. D. Lee Company; Miller Western Wear; Mr. Jean Myers; the Pinto Horse Association of America; Pioneer Wear, Inc.; The Rodeo Cowboys Association; The Stetson Hat Company; Levi Strauss and Company; Tex Tan Western Leather Company.

# Western Rider's Handbook

# WESTERN HORSES

The ideal Quarter Horse as interpreted by artist Orren Mixer. *Courtesy the American Quarter Horse Association.*

# The American Quarter Horse

The Quarter Horse was the first breed of horses developed in America. The Southern colonies, Virginia and the Carolinas, made horse racing the leading outdoor sport. These were short 440-yard dashes run on village streets or plantation lanes. The race was tagged the "quarter miler." Breeders began working toward producing a horse with just the right build for this match-racing preoccupation. The fine English Thoroughbred-type mares were crossbred to the stout war and work horses brought north by the Spanish. The result was a compact, stocky horse that could start quicker and run faster — for short distances — than any other breed. The quarter-mile running horse was born.

As the population pushed west, the Quarter Horse went along as a dependable, hard-working pioneer. The ranchers soon discovered this chunky little powerhouse had an instinct for working with cattle. His agility, small size and tractable temperament made him a natural for cattle drives, roundups and every other phase of demanding ranch work. The Quarter Horse had found a home.

The greatest concentration of this American horse breed remained in the Southwest until the founding of the first official breed registry,

The American Quarter Horse Association, in 1941. The first horse listed by the registry was a well-bred stallion named Wimpy. He was foaled in 1937 on the King Ranch in Texas. For the first time, organized, selective breeding information was available, and the breed spread rapidly across the country. The people of Canada, Mexico and even some countries overseas fell in love with one of the most versatile horses in the world.

A Quarter Horse is instantly recognizable by his body shape. He was originally a small horse — heavy but never clumsy, short but graceful. Recent breeding for show stock, however, is producing much larger animals than those of ten or fifteen years ago. He is heavily muscled, particularly in the hindquarters. This provides the strength for his unmatched maneuverability. That a Quarter Horse can "turn on a dime and give you nine cents change" is an appropriate if overused description. Many a good rider unfamiliar with the quickness of a

**Quarter Horses have natural cow sense and are easily trained for ranch work or working show classes. Notice the horse's front feet in relation to her hind feet, and how securely her attention is focused on the cow. Marion's Girl is ridden by Buster Welch. *Courtesy the American Quarter Horse Association.***

**Quarter Horses are the favorites of many for all-around Western-style pleasure riding.** *Courtesy the American Quarter Horse Association.*

well-trained Quarter Horse has been made painfully aware of his reining sensitivity.

This breed is also well respected for its disposition. Of course, personality differs from horse to horse, but generally the Quarter Horse is calm, intelligent, steady and willing. He is an excellent family pleasure horse. He is a cool-headed game horse. He is a reliable working horse, and he is a winning short-track race horse.

Naturally, a Quarter Horse's way of going is as unique as his appearance, because it is a direct result of his build. He has a low-headed, purposeful walk; a short, choppy, jogging trot; and a rather slow, easy, effortless lope. A practiced Quarter Horse can bound into a dead run from a standstill. He can thrust his power-packed hindquarters under him and slide to an instant stop. And anywhere in between, he can turn in any direction at any speed, with a minimum of signaling from his rider. He is usually quiet when he ought to be quiet and ready when he ought to be ready.

More and more Quarter Horses are being used for English-style riding. They are performing well. But the term Quarter Horse will always bring to mind the original Western horse. He was a race horse before he was a working horse. He was a cowboy's horse before he was a show horse. Today, he is all three. So, the next time someone quips, ''A Quarter Horse, huh? What's the other three quarters?'' Tell 'em, ''Speed, brains and heart!''

# 2

# The Appaloosa

The horse breed we know as the Appaloosa has been in existence since prehistoric times. These distinctively colored horses were drawn on cave walls in France. They appeared in Chinese art around 500 B.C. The Persians produced images of the spotted animals during the fourteenth century.

The Appaloosa's introduction to this continent is theoretical. Probably, they were imported from the Near East to Mexico around 1600. The Plains Indians spread northward, taking the rare, colorful horse with them. By the early 1700s, the Nez Percé Indians of the Northwest had become acquainted with the beautiful Appaloosa. They so admired this animal's intelligence, brilliant markings and stamina that they began a selective breeding program. The fertile bottomland of the Palouse River was ideal for horse production, so the animals became known as Palouse horses. "A Palouse" was slurred to "Apalouse," which next became "Apalousie." Finally, the spelling seems to have settled on "Appaloosa."

An Indian horse must be fast, hardy, intelligent and agile. The Appaloosa served his developers well. He rapidly became the favorite war and hunting horse. He was surefooted, able to stand the hardships of mountain riding and could endure long hours of hard work. Also, he was fast enough to fulfill the Indians' enjoyment of racing. He had a

**This Appaloosa has a rather large blanket. Notice how the spots diminish in size as they approach the withers. *Photo by Allen L. Bird, courtesy* Appaloosa News.**

pleasant disposition that made him an agreeable animal to have around camp.

Under the sharp eye of the skillful Indians, the Appaloosa was bred to near perfection. Then, after the shattering Nez Percé War of 1877, the breed almost disappeared. In desperate flight, Chief Joseph led his people on a 1,300-mile trek into Canada. The valiant spotted horses carried men, women, children, and household goods across the rugged Northwest, outrunning five United States armies. They would have reached safety except for the white man's gadgetry — steamboats and the telegraph.

Chief Joseph surrendered at the Bear Paw Mountains in Montana. From there, the tribe's magnificent animals were sold. Mixed breeding weakened the characteristics so finely developed and diluted the unique color schemes.

In 1938, the Appaloosa Horse Club was formed by a group of people determined to keep the famous Nez Percé horses from slipping away completely. A few known purebred descendants of the old Indian

Leopard coat patterns are the favorites of many Appaloosa owners. This horse also displays the heavy, powerful muscling
characteristic of the breed. *Photo by Allen L. Bird, courtesy*
Appaloosa News.

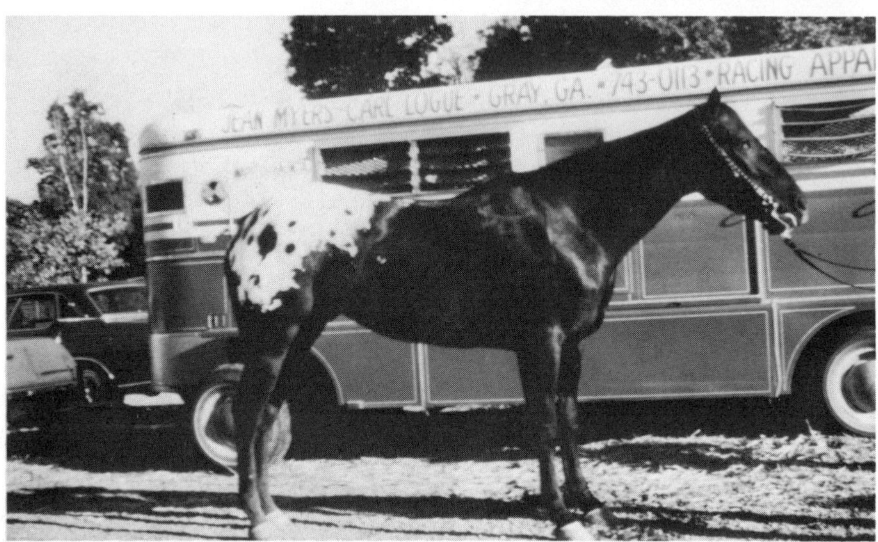

Rosie Leola, owned by Jean Myers of Gray, Georgia, displays a small, clearly defined blanket. Notice the "smoke rings," or areas of coloring around her dark spots.

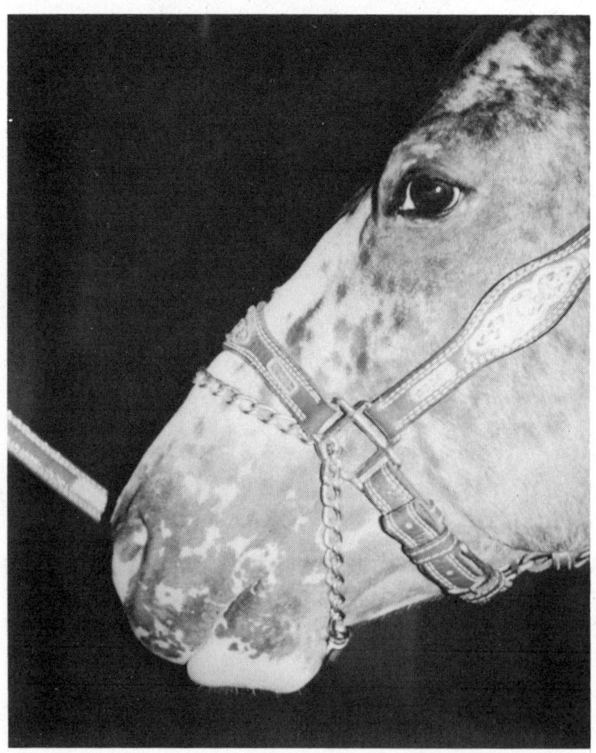

It's About Time shows the mottled skin coloring around a purebred Appaloosa's eyes and muzzle. This stallion is owned by Hidden Hills Farms in Knoxville, Tennessee.

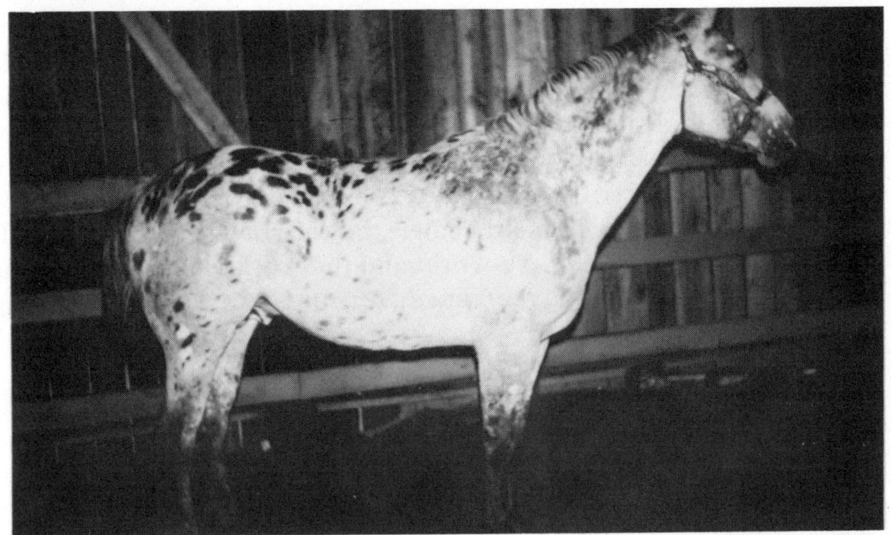

**Double Plaudit lives up to his high breeding by beautifully combining a blanket and all-over spotting. He is also owned by Hidden Hills Farms.**

bloodlines comprised the foundation stock. Today, the Appaloosa is again a finely bred, gentle, adaptable horse. Appaloosas make up one of the largest breed registries in the world, and it is still rapidly growing.

The Appaloosa is principally a Western horse, as his heritage would indicate, but the versatility of the breed is practically limitless. The familiar spots are as likely to be seen on an advanced jumping course as they are competing in an endurance trail ride. Appaloosas are sturdily built, learn quickly, and are easy to handle. That combination produces an exceptional stock horse, pleasure horse, or family pet.

Besides the varying spotted coats, Appaloosas have other identifying marks. The eye is encircled with white, much like a human's. The skin is irregularly mottled with black and white, particularly noticeable around the nostrils and lips. The hoofs have black and white vertical stripes.

No two coat patterns are identical. Most will be of a regular base color (bay, brown, black, sorrel, etc.) with a white "blanket" over the loin and hips containing round or oval spots. Some are a base color with contrasting spots over the hip area, but no blanket. Others, called leopard types, are spotted over their entire body, with the pattern more exaggerated across the hip area.

Except for his color scheme, the Appaloosa is a typical Western horse in every way. He moves through his gaits easily and quietly. He is level-headed and not easily excitable. He is highly intelligent, a good worker, and his disposition is superb. Many Appaloosas appear to have an almost instinctive orientation toward people. They make excellent youths' horses because they are kind and trustworthy. They are superior performing horses because they are flashy and talented. It is most fortunate for the horse world and the world of Western riding that the Appaloosas were reclaimed, regenerated, and are thriving today.

# 3

# The Arabian Horse

The number of Arabian horse fanciers is increasing greatly every year. Growth in the use and display of these unusual equines has brought a touch of glamour to the almost workaday world of Western riding. The Arabian horse admirably combines the pomp and splendor of a high spirit with the grit and determination of a skilled performer. He is regal and sophisticated, but he can work cattle like a hired hand. He is fancy and graceful, but he can dig in and get the job done — almost any job.

The breed name conjures up thoughts of a robed rider and bespangled horse dashing wildly across endless sand dunes. And the picture is fairly accurate. The Arabian was developed on the desert and lived closely with his nomad owners. It is this heritage that makes Arabian horses different physically and mentally.

The Arabian is fine-boned and delicate in appearance. While the bones are somewhat smaller than in other horses, they are denser and therefore stronger. He has a short, nearly level back and carries his **head and tail high and arched. The dished face and a wider than** average forehead provide a larger brain area.

Arabians are smart, inquisitive and personable. The nomads' habit of keeping the horses in their tents endowed the animals with a real affinity for human beings. Today, they are delightfully friendly crea-

**The classic Arabian pose shows off this breed's unique features. Notice the high, arched neck and tail, the dished face and the fine bone structure.** *Courtesy the International Arabian Horse Association.*

tures who seek a close association with people and seem to be especially fond of children. Arabian horses will play, much like dogs or other house pets. A ball, stick or any unusual object will get close scrutiny, then a gentle nudge with a curious nose. If it is movable, the horse will probably push it around. If it isn't, he's likely to paw it carefully. Any activity around Arabian horses will capture their interest and probably result in a nosy intrusion.

While they are easily controlled, these animals have an ebullient spirit. In most halter classes, the horses are expected, if not required, to stand quietly still. Not so in Arabian shows. The exuberant Arabs prance, dance and toss their heads, each determined to be a bigger showoff than his ring mates.

Their endurance is unsurpassed by any other breed, and there are

**Witezarif exemplifies the strength and stamina characteristic of the Arabian Horse breed. He won the arduous Tevis Cup 100-Mile-in-One-Day Endurance Race four years in a row, 1970-1973. His owner and rider is Donna (Mrs. Pat) Fitzgerald.** *Courtesy the International Arabian Horse Association.*

physiological reasons for this. Their wide, flaring nostrils can gulp in larger quantities of air. Arabians have larger lungs and hearts. They can work longer and harder on less food and water than is necessary for other horses. This breed was the foundation for the Thoroughbred race horse.

While the major horse colors are found within the breed, dramatic white or black Arabians depicted often in art are actually rather rare. They are more likely to be chestnut, bay or gray.

Napoleon rode an Arabian in his many conquests. A long-time choice of nobility, the first recorded purebred Arabian to enter America was Ranger. He arrived in Connecticut in 1765. General George Washington purchased the Magnificent stallion to improve his own stock. Later in the nation's history, Ulysses S. Grant rode an Arabian as he fought to preserve the Union.

Some believe the Arabian horse as a breed is nearly perfect and cannot be improved upon. His aristocratic air and startling wisdom.

The typical Western sliding stop is exhibited here by Rafsi, an Arabian owned by Bruce and Joanne Crockett of Allen, Texas. His abilities made him the National Champion Arabian Stock Horse in 1969. *Courtesy the International Arabian Horse Association.*

make him a favorite of all who get to know him. He is truly the horse of kings and generals. But he is just as truly the horse of ordinary men, women and children. He is a parade prince or a cow horse. The Arabian is whatever someone wants him to be.

**El Haji of Friendship Farms in East Moline, Illinois, indicates the versatility of Arabians by cutting cattle. At this point, Lee Caldwell is just along for the ride. *Courtesy the International Arabian Horse Association.***

**4**

# The Morgan Horse

In 1789, Justin Morgan moved from Massachusetts to Vermont, taking with him his scruffy, undersized colt, Figure. The Thoroughbred-Arabian cross grew to barely over fourteen hands and approximately 1,000 pounds. Deep, heavy muscles layered the slight but dense skeletal frame. It soon became obvious that more power had been built into the diminutive horse than any other New England had ever known.

As an adult, Figure was amazingly diverse. He was a hard worker, pulling loads no draft horses could budge. He was fleet-footed. He outran the fastest quarter-mile racehorses in Vermont. He was not only an everyday horse but a Sunday one, too. Always statuesque, head held high and luxuriously full mane and tail flowing, he was beautiful in harness. Some say he even bore a President in a parade.

The little bay stallion died a lonely work horse's death at about the age of thirty. He had bred area mares and had done his usual amount of work — that of two horses — through his twenty-eighth year. He had belonged to several owners, yet his passing was not mourned in the bleak Vermont farmland where young horses were necessary for making a living. But suddenly the memory of his life was thrust upon horsemen in every American colony.

**Unusual strength for moderate size characterizes the Morgan horse. This mare and foal beautifully exhibit the Morgan's conformation.** *Courtesy American Morgan Horse Association, Inc.*

Throughout the New England countryside, there were appearing strangely small but strong colts and fillies. Their distinctive appearance brought them.much attention. It was quickly noised about that the little ones belonged to and were exactly like "that Morgan horse." Figure became known only as Justin Morgan, and one of the world's most productive light horse breeds was off and running.

Morgan horses seemed to excel at everything they tried, and their breeding ability is legendary. They were winning harness horses. They were show-quality saddle horses. Morgans supplied foundation stock for Standardbred, Hackney, and Tennessee Walking horse breeds.

They served nobly on both sides during the Civil War, gaining fame by being the exclusive mounts of the dapper Vermont Cavalry. General William T. Sherman's flashy war horse was a Morgan.

After the Free Homestead Act of 1862, countless settlers began a westward journey'on or behind their Morgans. By 1880, the small horses were in almost every state or territory, still proving equal to all tasks and spreading their characteristics across a continent. More and

**Personality and performance make the Morgan Horse a favorite with Western riders.** *Courtesy American Morgan Horse Association, Inc.*

more horses appeared with clean, almost hairless fetlocks, full silky manes on thick, majestic necks, delicate heads with large alert eyes and tiny attentive ears. They had easy, animated gaits with surprising speed at any of them. They were endowed with a good disposition and seemingly boundless courage and persistence. All of this inevitably led them to the ranges and cattle ranches of the frontier.

Here, they were predictably proficient. Magic Morgan blood mingled with the Quarter Horses' and produced an outstanding cow horse. Today, Morgans are receiving more notice every year as top Western horses. They are rising contenders in cutting contests, roping events, and trail competition. In fact, Morgans are now among the leading challengers in all phases of Western riding. As a breed, they embody all the traits necessary for a genuine Western horse. As individuals, they offer strength, unequaled service and genuine Western friendship.

**5**

# Other Breeds for Western Riding

All the color registries, Paint, Pinto, Palomino and Buckskin, to name a few, contribute largely to the world of Western riding. Palomino and Buckskin coloring can appear on registered Quarter Horses, but there are also color registries by those names. Color registries were organized to provide for the continuation of good quality horses and desired colors.

The Palomino is the familiar golden horse so frequently seen in parades. His brilliant shining coat and dazzling flaxen or white mane and tail are a delight to see. There are numerous Palominos working and performing in the Western realm. The combination of a well-trained Western horse and Palomino coloring is a valuable one.

The Buckskin horse is generally considered a Westerner. He is sandy colored, usually with a black mane, tail and stockings. Some Buckskins have a black stripe, often called a mustang stripe, down the backbone. They are reminiscent of the early wild horses caught, broken and trained for range work.

The Paint and Pinto, favorites of the Indians, were indigenous to the West. It was only natural that the cowboys would capture them and put them to use as cattle horses. There are two main color types, *tobiano*

**Pinto horses were prized by the Indians. Their vivid coloring, such as on this tobiano, was thought to bring good fortune. *Courtesy the Pinto Horse Association of America.***

and *overo*. Tobianos are white with large, smooth areas of color on the head, upper neck, chest, flanks and tail. They almost always have white legs and white crossing over the backbone. Overos are a solid color with irregular patches of white along the midsection of the body on the neck, sides and flanks. They usually have solid-color legs, manes and tails and center backs. The basic coat colors are black, bay, or chestnut.

The term "Western horse" is a general one, referring more to the type of horse than to a particular breed. Breed registries were nonexistent for the early ranchers, so any horse that could do the job did it. While some breeds are synonomous with Western-style riding, it depends upon the individual horse. Regisitries and associations are

**Pamela Scott of Albuquerque, New Mexico, is a winner on Yes Mam, owned by Rusty and Diane Paris, Chino, California. Yes Mam is a beautiful example of an overo Pinto.** *Courtesy the Pinto Horse Association of America.*

greatly beneficial in improving and perpetuating quality bloodlines and colors. But registration papers can't cut cattle or lope on a loose rein.

Any horse can be ridden under a saddle with a horn on it. Any rider can put on a pair of high-heeled boots and get on him. Neither will necessarily be Western. There is much more to it than that. True Western horses are unique and recognizable. They are durable, agile and maneuverable. They are relatively small, yet strong and powerful. They are intelligent and even-tempered. They are quiet but not lazy, lively but not wild, steady but not dull.

Horsemanship of the seventies is demanding versatility from all breeds. Countless heretofore Western horses are sailing over fences or chasing hounds. Likewise, horses with no traceable cow-horse ancestry are successful in their new roles of trail riding or roping. From the prancing Arabian to the much loved backyard cow pony, horses all over the world are becoming, if only for several fun-filled hours a week, proud and skillful Western horses.

Part II

# WESTERN WEAR AND GEAR

**6**

# The Well-dressed Westerner

Tradition is the one and only dictator of today's Western wear. Necessity on the dusty, brushy, blazing hot or freezing cold ranges was the mother of this tradition. Fabrics had to be heavy and durable. Hats had to be sun shields, windbreakers and watering troughs. Boots were for walking, riding and plowing up the ground behind a brand-shy steer. Bandanas wiped away sweat and kept the cowboy from consuming a steady diet of dust and sand. Leather provided extra protection in gloves, chaps and jackets.

Much of the cowboy's ornamentation was developed from Mexican and Indian art. Their love for color and exquisite craftsmanship added much to Western garb. We are fortunate this influence has survived the years. The beautiful metalwork and stone inlays, the elaborate tooling and leather carving are re-created in belts, boots, buckles and jewelry.

The Westerner of today is a composite of cowboy, cattle baron and businessman. Western clothes are better fitting and more colorful than ordinary ones. The body-hugging tailoring and graceful lines are flattering to male and female wearers alike. But looks are only part of the picture. Western styles are comfortable, long-wearing and, in the long run, a practical addition to any wardrobe.

**Beautiful boots in all colors, styles and sizes are available to today's Westerners. Pocketbooks, belts, billfolds, even hair barrettes are closely coordinated in this Tony Lama collection. *Courtesy Tony Lama Company, Inc.***

## Boots

The early trail drivers wore boots with round toes and low, flat heels. The tops came up to just below the knee, the front halves of which were two separate pieces of leather. Decoration and stitching of the upper half was the predecessor to our fancy boot tops.

The narrow toe was instituted when it proved handier for poking into the stirrup in a hurry. Stirrups were also responsible for the development of higher heels. A cowboy mounting on the run could ram his foot into the stirrup and count on the heel to keep it from slipping through. As stirrups narrowed, heels moved farther forward on the boot soles. The resulting sharp slant at the back of the heel helped the cowboy with any wrangling he had to do on foot. It dug into the ground and served as a gripping scotch.

Rodeo contestants who needed to be able to run freely resurrected the lower heel. The ''dogger'' heel was less clumsy, but also necessitated wider stirrups. Now, boots are available in varying heel sizes and heights. There are hundreds of new styles to choose from every season. Boots continue as durable, functional footwear for the ranch hand as well as the drugstore cowboy.

***Courtesy Tony Lama Company, Inc.***

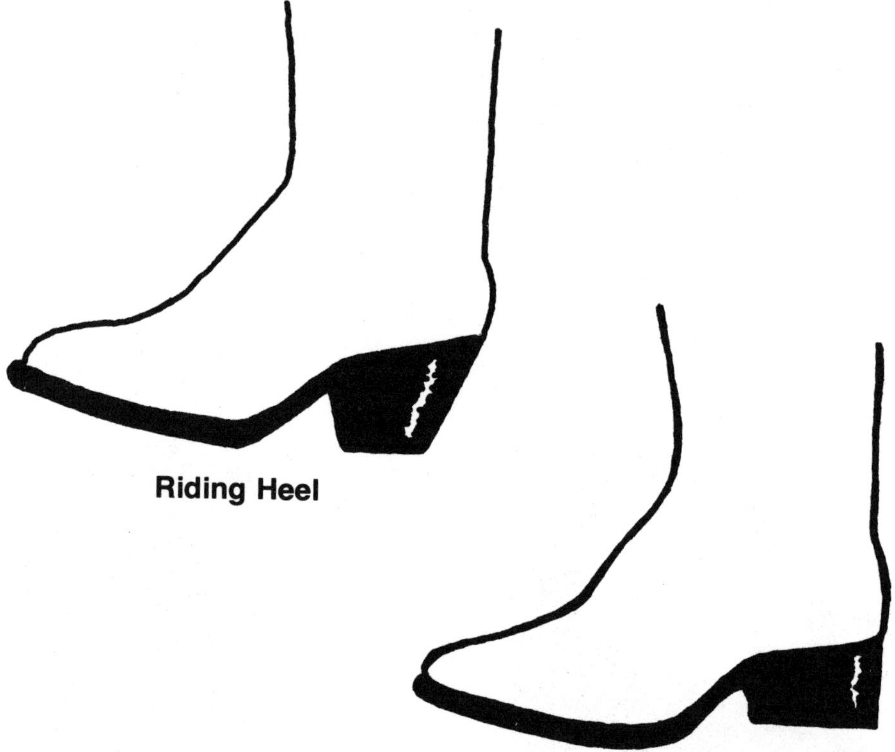

**Riding Heel**

**Walking or Dogger Heel**

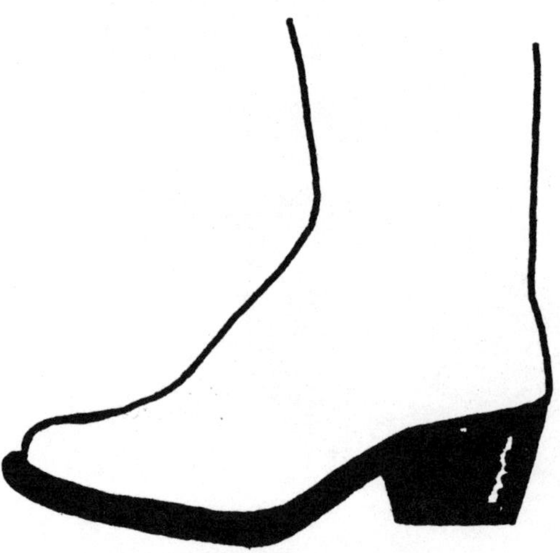

**Cowboy Heel**

**Cowboys of all ages appreciate the fit and serviceability of well-made Western casuals. *Courtesy Levi Strauss and Company.***

## Fashions

In the arena and out, cowboys and cowgirls are Western fashion plates. Jeans, the horse person's number one wardrobe staple, are no longer a monotonous blue. They are currently available in all colors, stripes, checks, trimmed and embroidered. The legs have flared, straight, or boot-cut bottoms. The boot-cut is a slight flare at the bottom of the pants leg, with the back of the leg longer than the front.

**Style and graceful lines make ladies' Western clothes some of the most attractive fashions available. *Courtesy H. D. Lee Company.***

*Courtesy Pioneer Wear, Inc.*

Multihued or solid shirts and blouses are coordinated with the slacks. Fabrics and prints are mixed, and variations of the old-time yokes are imaginative. The white cotton cowboy shirt is still seen, but color predominates. For appearing in shows, sleeves remain long and, in some ladies' styles, they are much fuller than normal.

**Photo by Len Foster, courtesy Miller Western Wear.**

Sleeveless vests are popular toppers with the ladies, but the tailored suit remains a favorite of both men and women for dressy occasions. Waist-length jackets are migrating from the purely work-clothes category to the casual.

**Western clothes are becoming a trend throughout the country. Leisure suits such as this one are the pacesetters of men's fashions.** *Courtesy Pioneer Wear, Inc.*

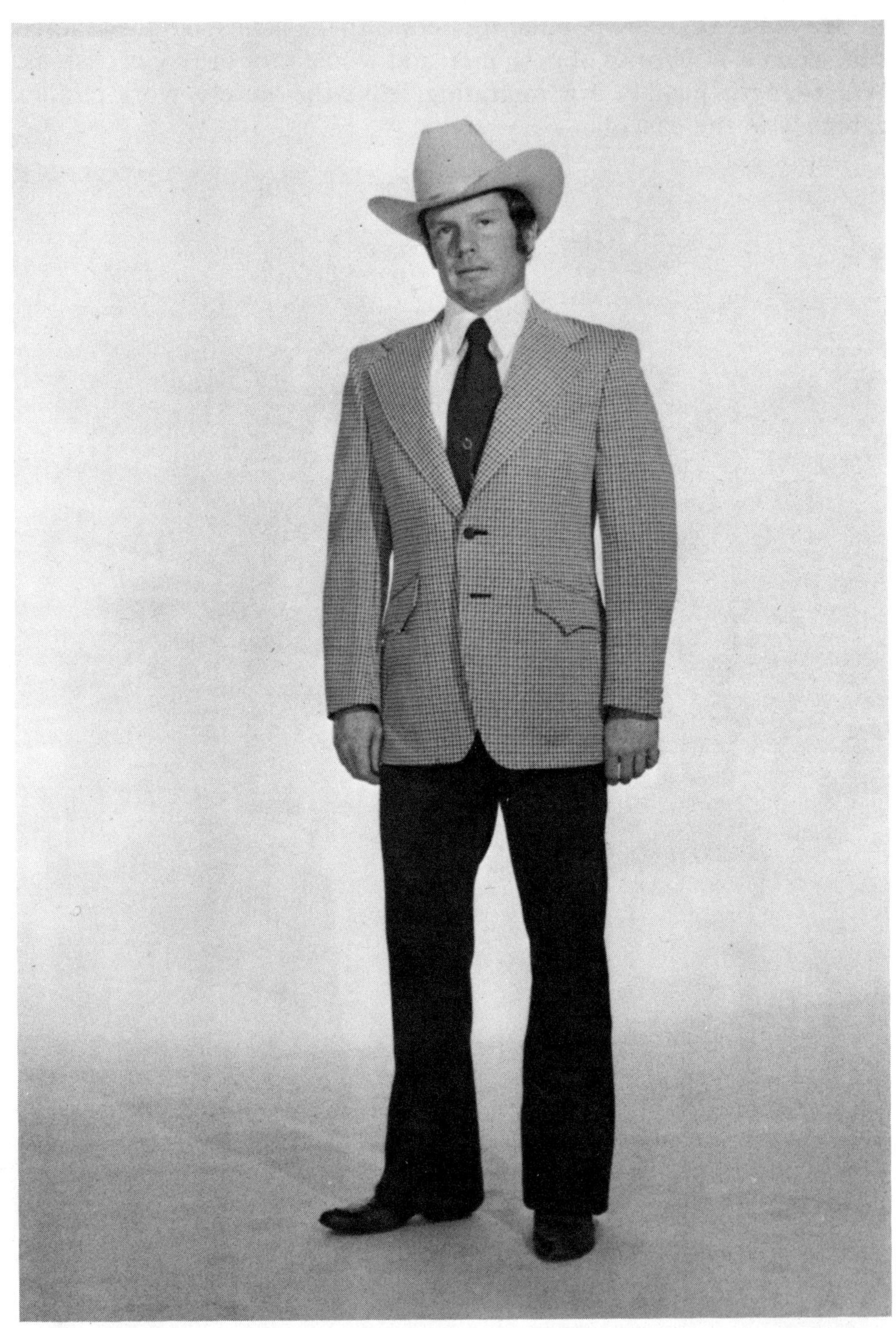

*Photo by Len Foster, courtesy Miller Western Wear.*

*Photo by Len Foster, courtesy Miller Western Wear.*

**Accessories**

A cloth tie, scarf or string tie is necessary for a completed outfit. The scarves are carried over from range-riding days when it was as valuable an item as a cowboy's hat. They are flashy and usually color keyed to the shirt and pants. The string or bolo ties or cloth ties are considered more dressy than the neckerchief. Some Westerners still sport the stockman's tie, a little cloth band which fits snugly under the collar. It often crosses at the throat and is secured with a stickpin.

The world of hats has become as diverse as other areas of Western clothing. They come in all colors in men's, women's and children's sizes. Straws are mainly summer hats and felts are designed for winter. However, both can be seen in the arena in any season. Nearly every hat company offers several crown shapes from the ten-gallon "Hoss" hat to the horseshoe crease.

**The Stetson Hat Company has been manufacturing cowboys' head-savers for 110 years. "The Revenger" was made by special request for William Holden for the movie *The Revengers. Courtesy Stetson Hat Company.***

Western belts and buckles are wider, thicker, heavier and more exquisite than any other style. Tooled and buckstitched belts, also available in colors, add a finishing touch as only leather can do. Some cowfolks sport their name tooled on the back of a belt, while others prefer plain leather, fancy stitching or intricate tooling.

Chaps are another of the accessories which have endured since they were routinely needed. The Mexican vaquero is credited with originating them. They draped two pieces of cowhide from the saddle horn and wrapped them around their legs. The leather protectors fended off biting briars and miles of clawing scrub brush. Now, they are available in colors and with decorative stitching. Some hug the leg closely, others flare slightly, and occasionally a pair of "bat wing" chaps will appear. These have widely cut, usually rounded, bottom edges. The back part of the legging is secured to the front half by metallic conchos, snaps or zippers. **The wearer buckles them on with a decorative belt** sewn to the top of the chaps. Brush-poppin' or show-hoppin', chaps are an integral part of the Western wardrobe of the seventies.

Most associations sponsoring shows do not dictate every item of clothing to be worn by contestants. Most do have some basic requirements, however. A Western hat and cowboy boots are usually stipulated, with chaps left to the option of the rider. Serious exhibitors make

**Western wear manufacturers have for many years attentively combined practicality and beauty. The result continues to be top-quality, high-style clothing. *Courtesy Tony Lama Company, Inc.***

every effort to present a complete but practical Western appearance. Attractive, conservative Western dressers command more attention and respect than do gaudy, outlandish clotheshorses.

When dressing for casual Western pleasure riding, select comfortable, serviceable garments. When dressing to show in Western classes, observe all rules of the specific show, including those of what to wear.

**7**

# Saddles and Bridles

## Saddles

Today's Western saddle is a several-centuries-removed modification of the early Spanish saddle used during the time of the Crusades.

The Conquistadors brought the saddle characterized by a padded seat and long stirrups to the New World. The introduction of Spanish longhorn cattle led to changes by the Mexican vaquero. The American stock saddle then evolved from the vaquero's, when the cowboy crossed paths with his south-of-the-border counterpart around 1850.

While the Southwestern cowpunchers retained much Spanish influence in their saddles, the American method of working cattle called for a few more changes. Spanish rigging had only one cinch, located directly under the pommel. Naturally, this was inadequate for heavy roping, so a back cinch was added. In California, however, the girth was simply moved back toward the cantle. This three-quarter-rigged saddle is still considered California equipment.

The "tree" of a saddle, or the foundation upon which it is built, is important in determining its quality. A hastily or poorly constructed tree will result in a warped or broken saddle which cannot or should not be used.

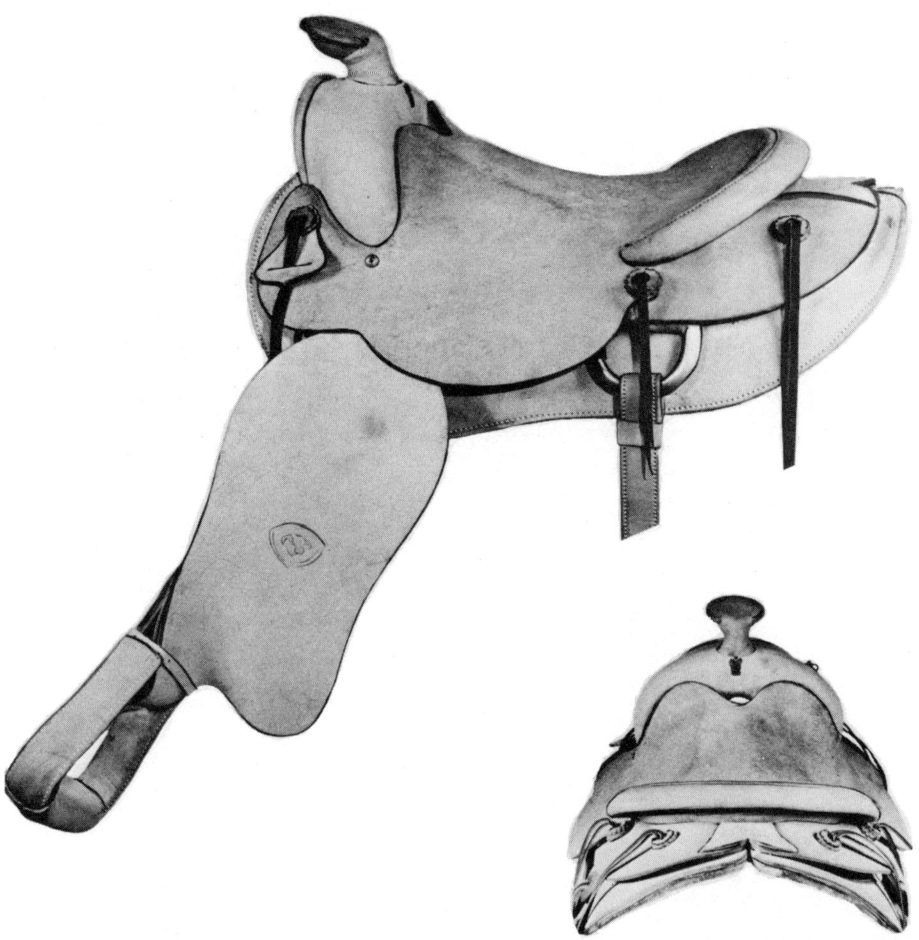

**A slick leather saddle with no padded seat is still the choice of many exhibitors and working cowhands. *Courtesy Tex Tan Western Leather Company.***

The early Texas as well as Mexican saddle trees were carved out of one piece of wood. This was usually a seasoned, well-dried log of elm, cottonwood or ash. To this day, there are some Mexican saddles with trees, horn and all, hand-carved out of one piece of wood. But the skill and time involved in such an operation led to the development of a simpler and faster method of construction.

Most saddle trees now consist of four pieces. The fork determines the width; two back pieces determine the length; and the raised, curved rear section called the cantle varies in height, curvature, etc. All these segments are put together with screws. The entire tree is then

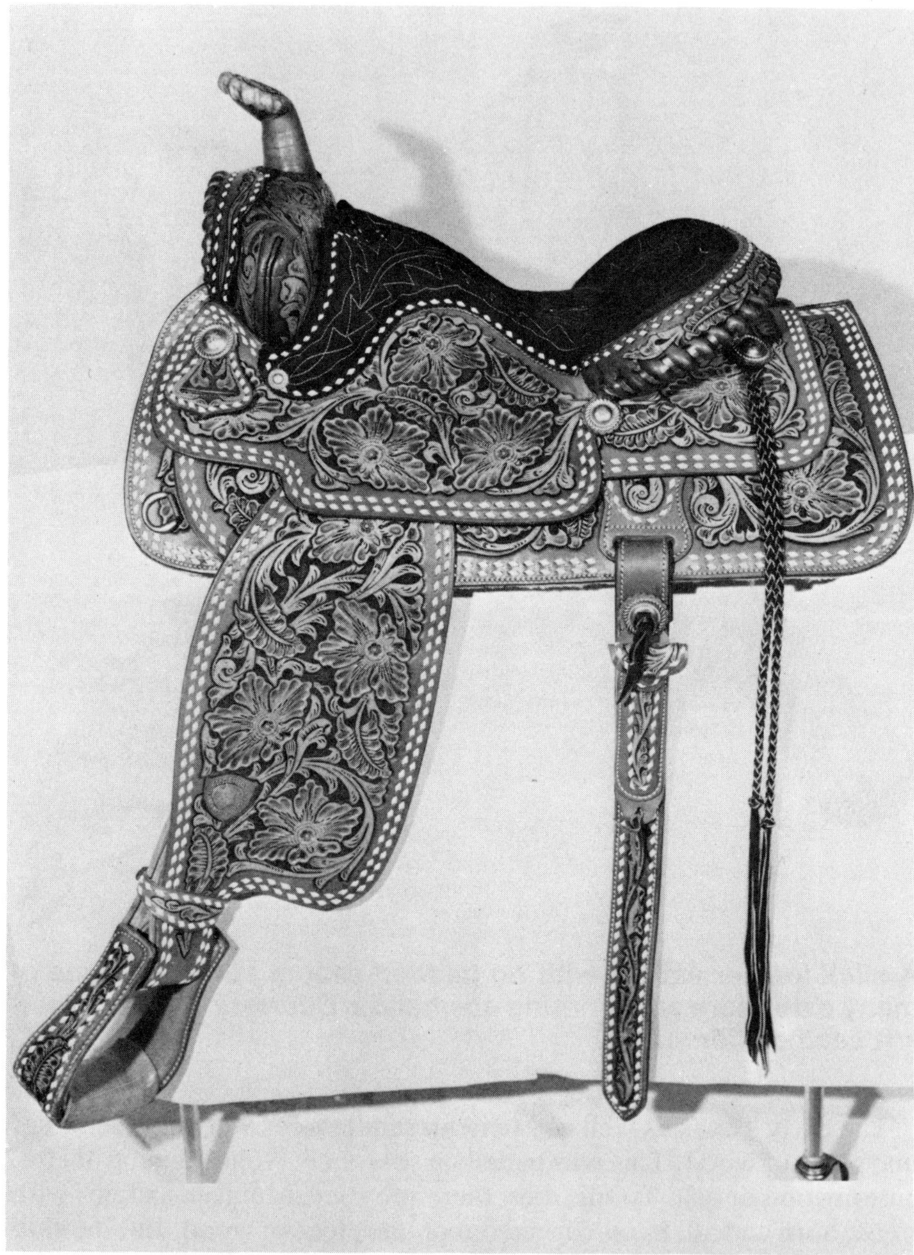

**Extensive padding, carving and stitching help make a good quality saddle attractive as well as serviceable** *Courtesy Tex Tan Western Leather Company.*

covered with wet rawhide, preferably steer or bull hide, fitted closely and stitched securely. The shrinkage of drying rawhide virtually molds the tree parts into one. Its strength matches any wood.

Cinching with one strap at the front of the saddle was adequate for most ordinary riding situaitons. But rough terrain and rougher work proved more than a single cinch could handle. A full double rig was the obvious answer to the working cowhand's dilemma — how to stay off his horse's ears with a 600-pound steer dancing on the end of a rope tied to his saddle. Keeping the rear of the saddle down was absolutely necessary.

This second cinch is drawn snug against the horse's belly, but *not tight*. Some riders allow it to hang slightly below the horse's flesh, so it won't touch him until it is needed. A happy medium must always be struck in fastening the back cinch. Too tight will be a constant annoyance, making the horse kick or stomp. Too loose will be a hazard

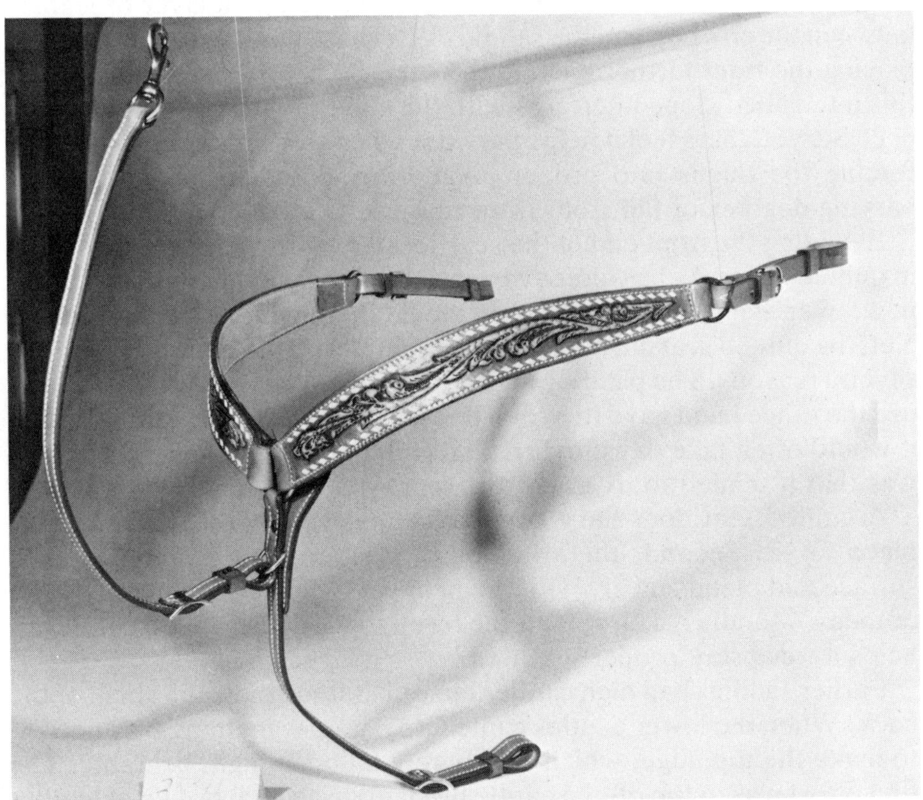

**Useful and ornamental, a breast strap completes a Western outfit.**
*Courtesy Tex Tan Western Leather Company.*

for snagging on underbrush or catching the horse's foot if he kicked at flies or fell.

There is one more thing to remember when using a double-rigged saddle. Often a rider can be in such a hurry to unsaddle, he or she will jerk the front cinch loose, forget the back one, and start pulling the saddle off. Ol' Bob either stands patiently while the saddle is replaced and the job is finished, or finishes it himself in a stomping, tree-busting, strap-breaking rage.

While the double-rig saddle leads in popularity, it is not really imperative for the pleasure rider. The three-quarter rig will do a good job of keeping the saddle in place, even over irregular landscape. (Breast straps and breeching should be used if riding up or down excessively steep hills continuously.) The location of the three-quarter cinch strap is such that it is comfortable for the horse, holds the saddle securely across the withers and augments the saddle's natural center of gravity.

The old Western saddle's seat fell slightly from the pommel toward the cantle. There were only a layer of bull hide and a layer of leather between the cowboy and the saddle tree. These days, the rise is higher, placing the rider farther back in the seat. Some professionals believe this intensified slope interferes with the ability to move forward when necessary. Others feel it helps the rider when working at high speed by forcing the thighs into proper position. Saddles are available with varying degrees of fall from front to back.

Elevating the front end of the seat seemed to bring about an upsurge in quilted seats. As has already been stated, the padded saddle was not new, even when it showed up on stock equipment in the late 1800s. Yet, the quilted seat did not become popular with old-time cowboys for several reasons. The padding and stitches could not withstand the hard use the range hand gave it. When the seat got wet during rain or snow, it would often take days to dry. The padding's other major drawback was that it tended to overheat the seat — the cowboy's, that is!

A quilted seat does have some advantages. Obviously, it is a soft place to sit. Second, the stitching is prettier than a smooth, slick surface and blends nicely with the heavy tooling and ornamental look of today's saddles. Third, with the trend toward low, rolled cantles, it helps a rider stay properly seated.

Earlier saddles had high cantles curved as if to cradle the small of the back. When the lower cantles came into being, something was needed to make the top edge, which was barely tailbone high, bearable. The first effort was to top off the cantle by slanting an inch or two of leather away from the rider. Theoretically, this occurred in Cheyenne, Wyoming. The town loaned its name to the new design, and there are few saddles manufactured today without a ''Cheyenne roll.''

The saddle horn, a roping cowboy's finger-saver, grew from a useless little knob atop the front of early Spanish saddles. There was no indication the Spaniards ever used a rope for anything, so it must have been ornamental.

The horn was often carved from the piece of wood which formed the saddle tree's fork. The slender, small heads would break off under stress. An oval of wood was left on the top for added strength. Iron and steel were finally used to reinforce the wooden horns. Some manufacturers experimented with nickel or brass horns. But uncovered metal proved too slick to be satisfactory for roping.

Saddle horns are another of the many variables of the modern Western saddle. They can be tall and slender or short and thick. The tops are small rounded mounds or five-inch-wide flat saucers. But whatever the appearance, there are jobs only a saddle horn can do. The toughest one by far is being a roper's snubbing post. When a saddle horn stops a 250-pound calf running ten feet ahead of the roper, it sustains over 1,000 pounds of jerk. Larger steers can exert as much as 3,000 pounds of yank.

The Western saddle was for years, and still is in some cases, home on the hoof for many a cowboy. It had to fit the horse right, and it had to fit the cowboy right. It endured all nature's elements and still took the punishment only ranch hands and range cattle could give it.

While the majority of Western saddles bought now will not be called upon to perform such arduous tasks, there are still important considerations to be made when selecting one. Comfort for horse and rider and purpose should be highest on the priority list.

The fork should rest solidly on the horse's withers, with the horn directly over and well above their highest point. If the fork is too broad, the saddle will ride the backbone. If it is too narrow, it will perch painfully high on the shoulders. A saddle that is too long for a horse's back will be irritating to the sensitive kidney area. And one that is too short will not only look like a wart on a pickle, but will be generally irritating at its pressure points.

A rider in a wrong saddle can be just as uncomfortable as a horse under one. The saddle should *feel* comfortable when the rider is seated forward in the seat with feet hanging freely, not in the stirrups. If the seat is too wide, it will be exhausting to ride and will interfere with proper weight distribution in the feet. If it is too narrow or too round, it will be difficult to stay well seated. The slope in the new padded saddles can also be a deciding factor. Can the rider *stay* in the right

## A Basic Stock Saddle

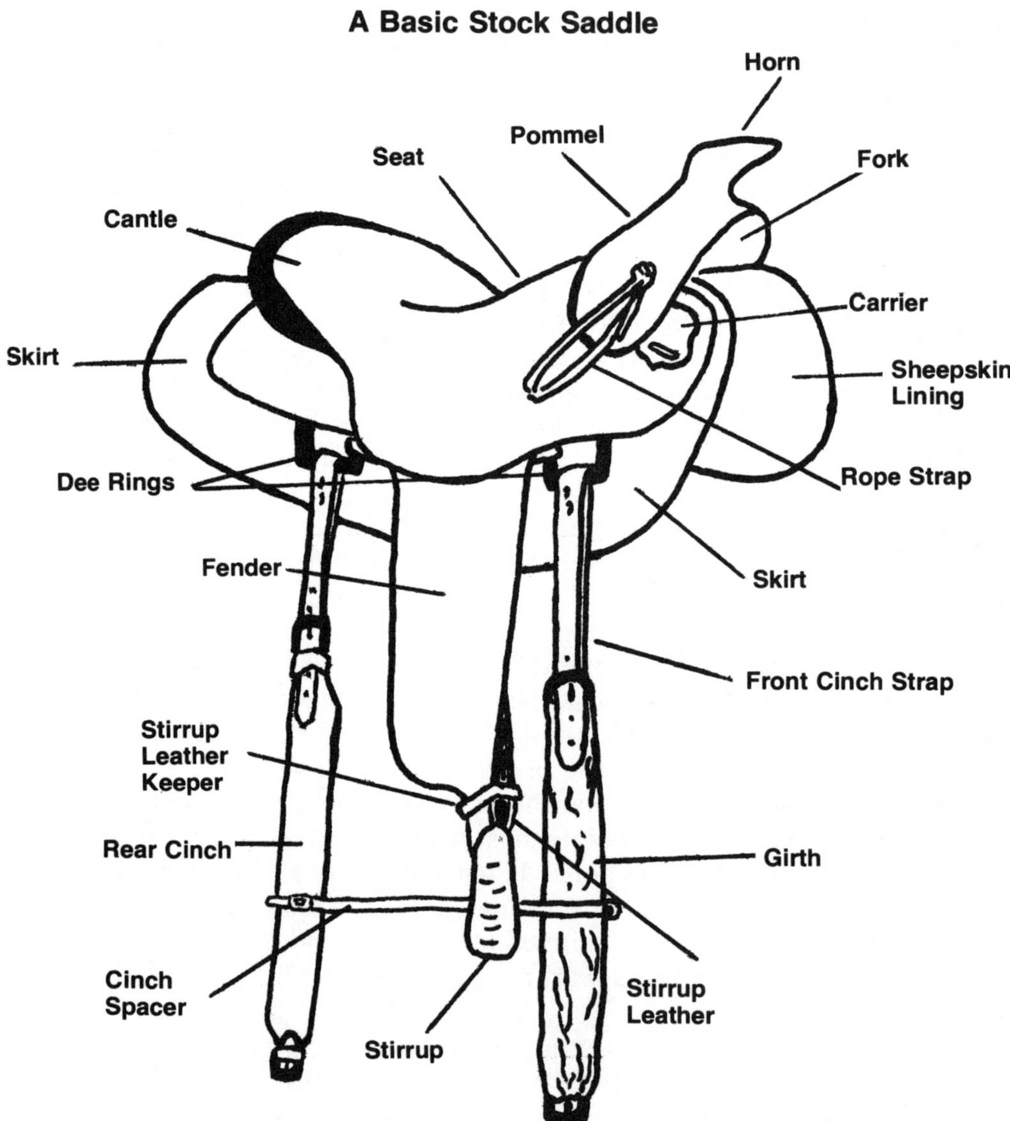

place in the seat for proper balance? A new Western rider in a poorly fitting saddle will be the first to declare the nickname "tender*foot*" has been misplaced by several inches!

All things considered, the Western saddle has evolved to its present state toward a most practical goal — maximum service with maximum comfort. The cowboy's needs were unique, but American pioneer ingenuity kept carving, tanning and stitching until those needs were successfully met.

## Bridles

Western riders have a wide range of bridle types from which to choose. A favorite training bridle, the hackamore, is another gift from our Spanish predecessors. In fact, the word *hackamore* is the cowboy term for the Spanish word *jáquima*. It is a simple bridle constructed of rawhide, leather, rope or any combination of the three. Its relative lack of irritation makes the hackamore a useful training tool.

A basic hackamore consists of a thin, single strap adjustable headstall, a bosal (noseband) and reins. The bosal is hard, rigid and usually made of rawhide with the reins attached at the back. Reining action works on the front of the nose as well as the lower jawbones.

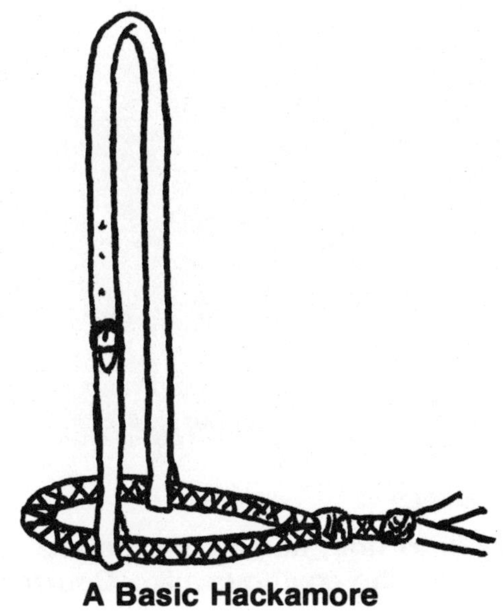

**A Basic Hackamore**

**Simple bridles with fine, narrow straps are often the choice of exhibitors and working cowboys alike. *Courtesy Levi Strauss and Company.***

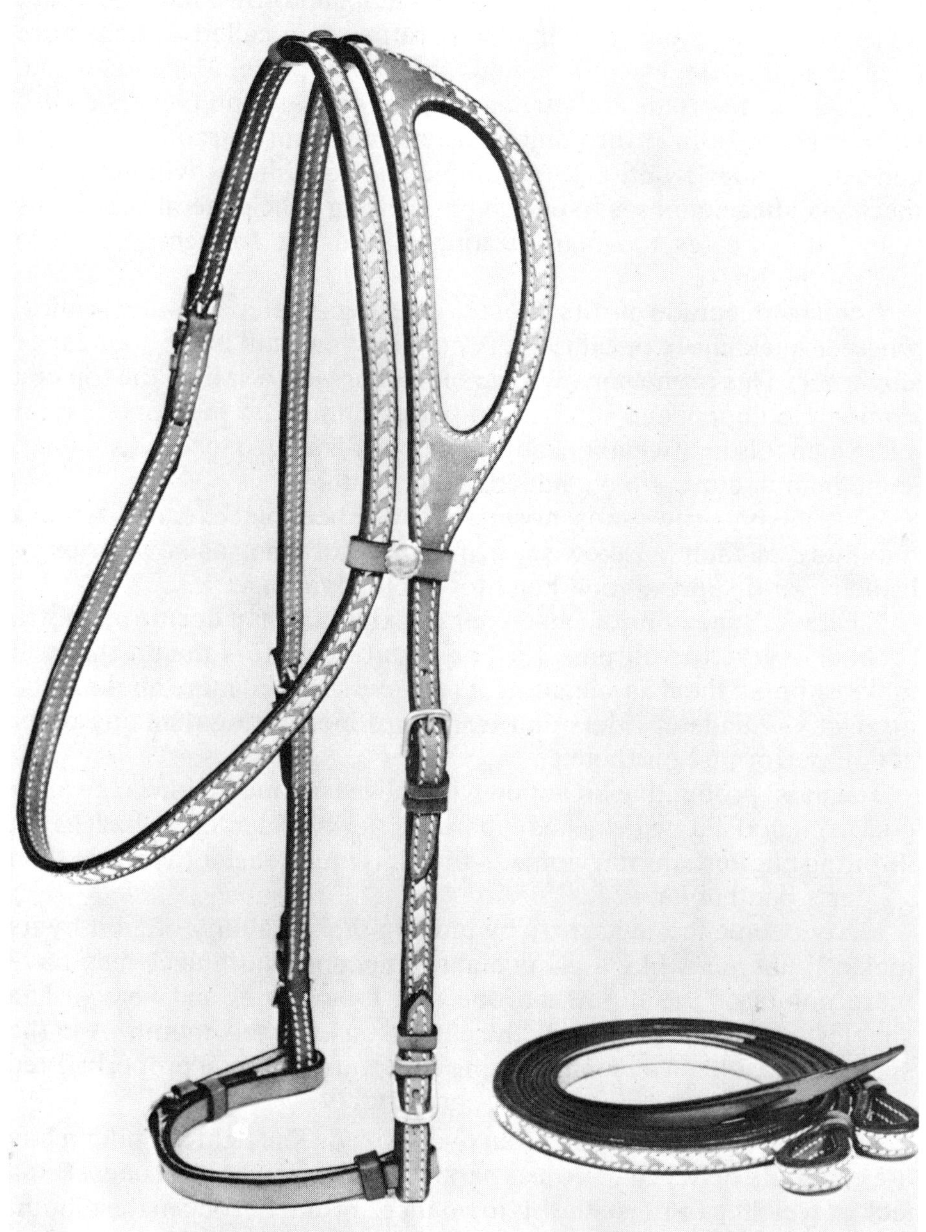

**This one-ear bridle is easy to use, lightweight and exquisitely crafted.** *Courtesy Tex Tan Western Leather Company.*

There are several variations of the hackamore-type bridle. Some employ a mouthpiece in addition to the bosal. Others are fashioned from rope, and still others add a throatlatch and browband. There are mechanical hackamores with an apparatus often called a hackamore bit. It is a metal device with a removable mouthpiece. Made much like a regular bit, the reins are attached to two shanks, and there is a curb strap. Reining utilizes the combined action of a curb strap, a noseband and, at the rider's option, a mouthpiece. Most shows will not allow mechanical hackamores to be used in the ring. The general consensus is that it indicates too many trappings and not enough training to control the horse.

Aside from parade outfits, most Westerners prefer slim-line bridles, whether hackamore or bit type. A popular headstall is the split ear or single ear. This is one narrow strip of leather with a split in the top or a semi-circle appendage stitched on to accommodate the horse's right ear. Since this lightweight headgear can be dislodged by head slinging, some manufacturers have added a throatlatch.

Wide, heavy browbands, nosebands and cheekpieces can cover up a multitude of faults. Likewise, a minimum of fine, narrow strips of leather can display a good head to much advantage.

Whatever type of bridle an owner or exhibitor may decide upon will probably serve the purpose for horse and rider. It is the bit that will make or break them as a team. Horses have suffered more abuse at the insensitive hands of riders and from improper bitting than any other action performed on them.

The most productive bit action with the least hand action is the main goal. A good bit with a heavyhanded, jerky rider is as bad as an ill-fitting bit. Perhaps it's worse — the bit is much easier to change than a rider's bad habits.

Many people are led astray by judging the suitability of a bit by its looks. What *looks* like a lightweight, innocent mouthpiece may have more points of irritation than one that *looks* cruel and heavy. The simplest bit is not necessarily the easiest on a horse's mouth. And the spade bit, a rather awesome-looking contraption, can, if properly fitted and handled with respect, work comfortably.

Weight is a consideration often overlooked. The light aluminum bits are generally believed to be less harsh than the iron or steel ones. But a lack of weight can cause the bit to bounce around or rock in the mouth. This in turn will call for more and heavier reining action from the rider. The lighter bits require more pressure for necessary communication. In contrast, heavier bits tend to be stabilized in the mouth by their own weight. It takes little pressure on a heavy piece of metal to relay the proper signals.

By far, the most important aspect of a bit is its design. A poorly designed bit will produce a horse whose mouth is so miserable he couldn't concentrate on anything else if he wanted to. The word ''severe'' is not always synonomous with ''cruel.'' Some horses require a severe bit. But a properly designed severe bit will not cut the bars, tear the lips, pinch the cheeks, rub the chin or choke the horse. Severity is determined by the type and amount of metal necessary in the horse's mouth for good control. Severity need not result in pain or damage.

The simple, true snaffle is a fairly innocent, usable bit, frequently used in breaking horses. Since Western horses are trained to respond quickly and sharply to the reins, a snaffle bit is usually abandoned when a green horse has become accustomed to being controlled by his mouth.

There is a snaffle which is frequently confused with the regular one and therefore falsely considered innocent. This is called a Western curb with a broken mouth. The joint in the center will rise, and the ends of the bit come down at a harsh angle on the bars. All the pressure occurs here, since the tongue can offer no support. In conjunction with a chin strap, the horse's mouth is put in a painful vise every time pressure is applied.

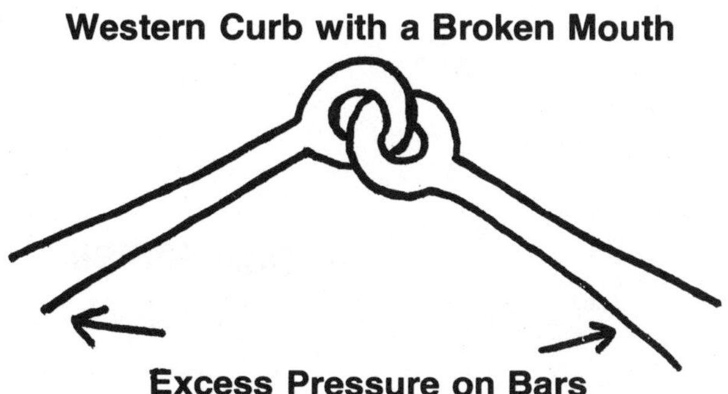



Another bit with a deceivingly mild appearance has a slightly curved bar. Here again, the weight of the bit rests on the outside edges of the bars. Naturally, the pressure increases with rein usage.

The true straight bar bit, however, is easier on the mouth. The lack of curve in the straight bar shifts a good deal of weight onto the tongue, relieving the sensitive bars. This increased tongue pressure might encourage a horse to open his mouth excessively, particularly with a heavy-handed rider.

The most commonly used good performance bit is one with a low

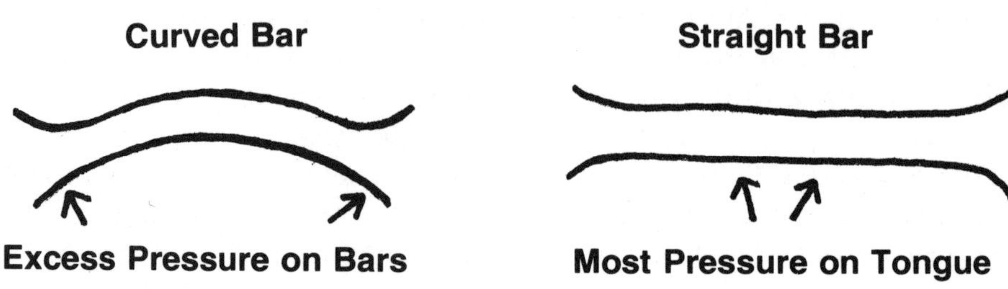


port. The gentle curve in the center of the mouthpiece and the level ends conform comfortably to the shape of a horse's mouth. There is equal pressure transmitted to tongue and bars. A higher port bit still puts some weight on the tongue but rides more heavily on the bars.

To compensate for a thin mouthpiece, some riders wrap it with tape, rubber, etc., in a feeble effort to protect the horse's mouth. Uneven wrapping and frayed or aging ridges will do much more harm than good.

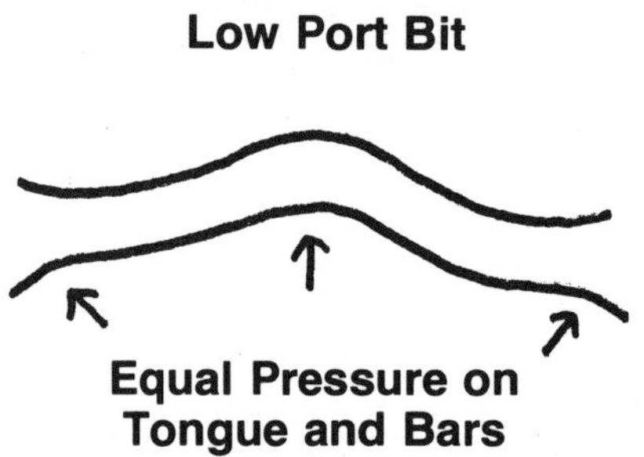


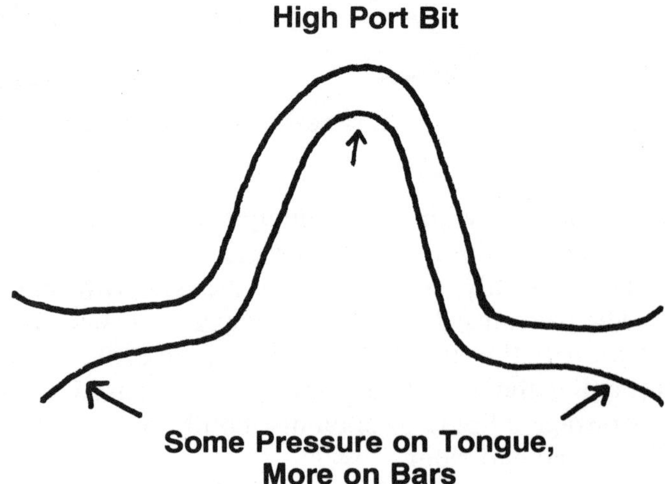

Crickets, the small, rotating spheres sometimes inserted in the ports of bits, are controversial. Some riders like them, some don't. Some crickets hurt, proper ones won't. The best cricket will nearly fill the space of the port. These larger ones allow proper tongue pressure, roll freely and do not pinch the tongue.

**Cricket**

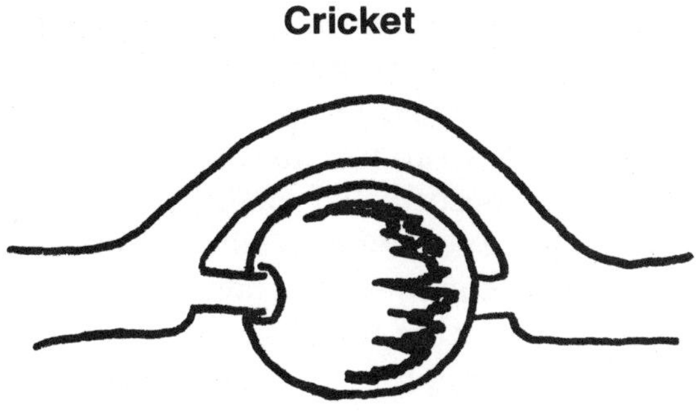

**Roller Nearly Fills Port**

Successful use of a spade bit requires precision training and feather-light hands. This bit is of Spanish ancestry and is still seen most among California riders. It consists of a cricket and flat spade-shaped disc mounted onto the center of a straight bar mouthpiece. Sometimes there is a chain from the spade to the ends of the mouthpiece. Again, when the horse is familiar with it and a rider understands it, a spade bit performs well. Otherwise, it can completely mutilate a mouth.

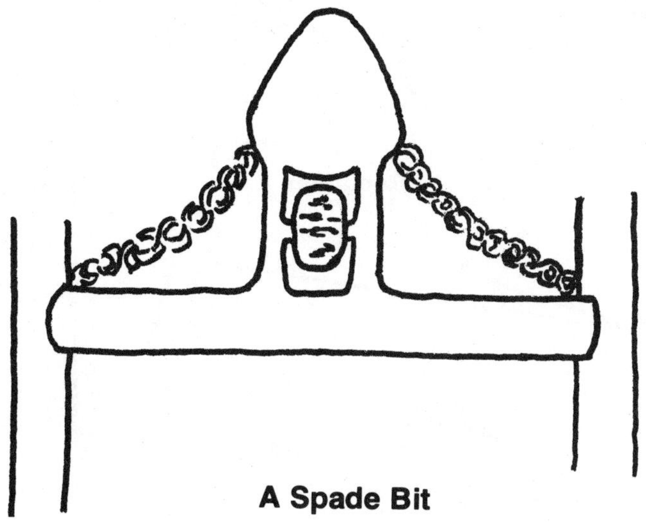

**A Spade Bit**

Mouthpieces are not the only factors determining the severity of a bit. The shanks and curb strap or chain dictate the leverage exerted on the mouth. A snug curb strap will relay the force promptly when the reins are pulled. The proportionate length of the shank to the overall length of the bit will determine how much the reins are pulled before the mouth is pressed. For example, if the mouthpiece occurs halfway between the connections for the reins and the headstall, leverage is decreased. If the shank is longer from the mouthpiece to the reins, leverage is increased and less reining is needed to activate the bit.

Preferences vary between curb straps and curb chains. Leather straps will stretch when wet, so conscientious attention must be given to regular adjusting. A properly fitted chain, one which will lie uniformly flat, does well. However, when a curb chain is attached to the bit by small leather straps, pinching and chafing can occur to the chin and lip corners. The best location for either curb strap or chain is an additional loop behind and below the headstall connection.

## A Basic Curb Bit

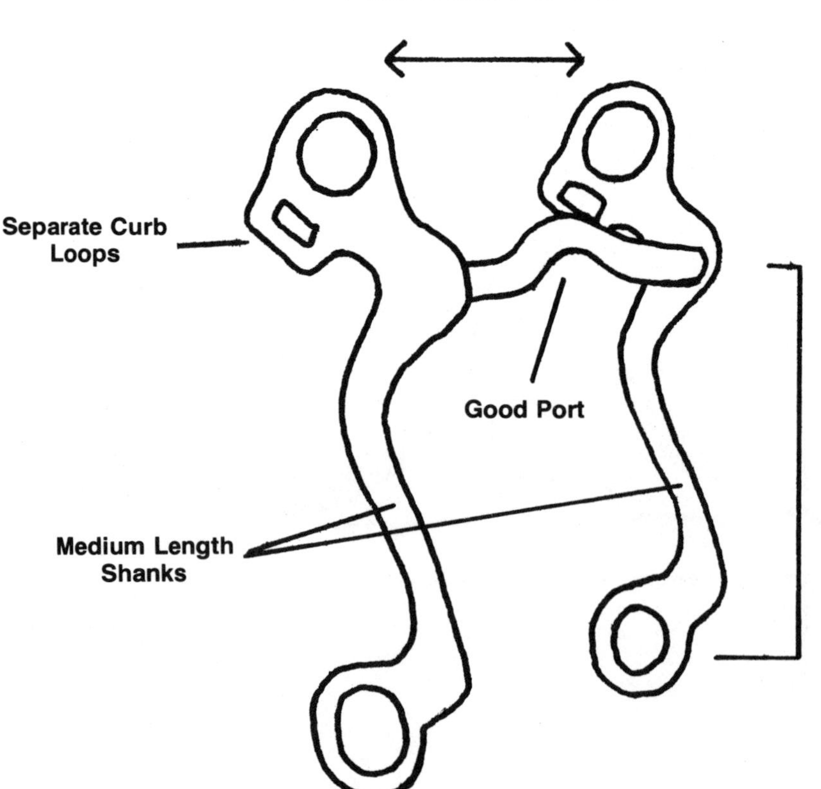

The better-quality bits slant outward at the headstall end. Logically, this effort at following the head's natural contour alleviates unnecessary gouging and rubbing.

Countless unfortunate horses return from every ride with bleeding lips, raw bars or both. It is no wonder they avoid the bit and protest the reins with poor mouth and head habits. Carelessness or callousness on the owner's part is solely responsible for such needless misery. A basic knowledge of bits and sensitivity to a horse's discomfort is needed to decide on the correct mouth gear.

# 8

# Miscellaneous Equipment

Horse equipment falls generally into two main categories — necessity or luxury. Necessities keep horse and rider safe and comfortable. Luxuries add to appearance or convenience. With the endless varieties of horse equipment available to today's rider, neither appearance nor convenience need be sacrificed for the other.

Of course, a saddle blanket or pad is used to protect a horse's back. Especially tender horses or those with a sharply slanting back or prominent withers may require a combination of the two. Both are made in attractive colors and designs.

Halters can be anything from a couple of loops in a rope to bring Ol' Bob in from the pasture to a heavily tooled, buck-stitched leather showpiece. The halters with snaps just below the ear are much more convenient than the older ones which buckle.

The jet age has given us nylon halters in bright colors. They are lightweight, won't rot, and are guaranteed unbreakable. The last characteristic suggests a horse should not be turned out to pasture or neglected for long periods of time when wearing one. It could be a tragic source of accident. If a horse became securely entangled and panicked, nylon halters will not break. The same is true with some thickly layered and heavily stitched leather ones. Most ordinary leather halters will allow a ring or strap to yield to excessive thrashing

**Thick, heavy saddle pads and/or blankets are necessary for safe, comfortable, proper saddling. Inadequate padding will result in a horse's painful or injured back.** *Courtesy Tex Tan Western Leather Company.*

**While hobbles won't necessarily keep a horse in one place, they help cut down on his wandering room. They should be smooth and nonchafing.** *Courtesy Tex Tan Western Leather Company.*

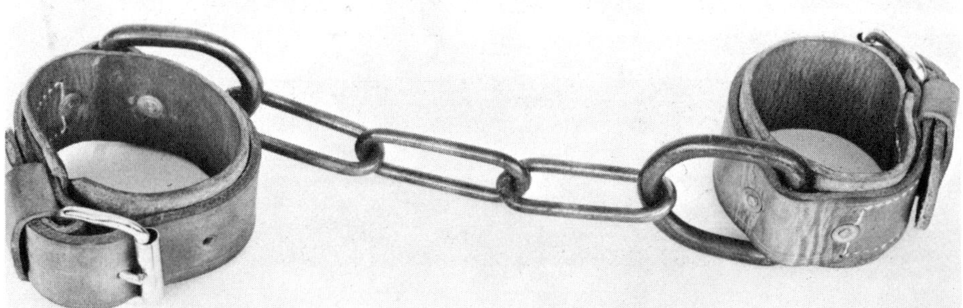

or pulling. In certain circumstances this could save a horse's life.

Shin boots or skid boots protect horses' legs from a number of injuries. The ranch horse or the working performer can suffer numerous cuts and scrapes. Sliding stops will skin the rear fetlocks. Fancy footwork provides ample opportunity for self-inflicted wounds to ankle and leg bones.

For the rider, there is an endless list of miscellanies. One of the most important take-alongs is rain gear. A slicker, poncho or rider's raincoat is not only good sense on a trail ride, it is frequently required in some show classes.

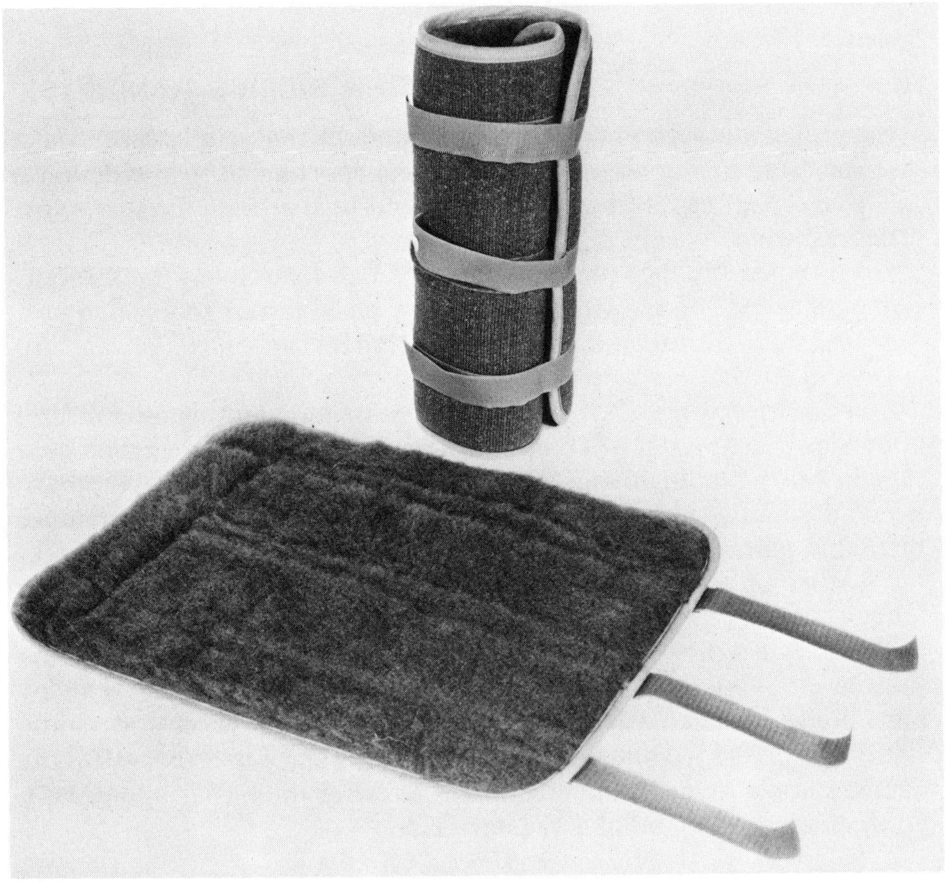

"No foot, no horse" the old adage says, and it is true for the legs, too. Protective bandages and skid boots prevent numerous unnecessary leg injuries. *Courtesy Tex Tan Western Leather Company.*

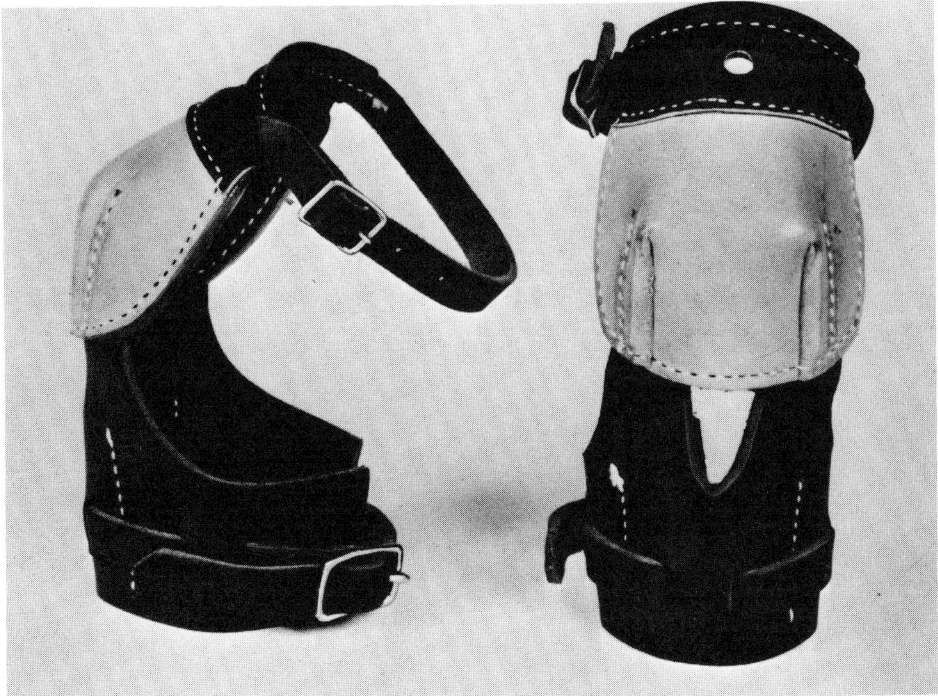

Several manufacturers offer handsome saddlebags and cantle pockets. These are handy on long rides for transporting small incidentals.

There are all types of quirts, crops and leather bats for that extra little incentive.

Hoof picks, brushes and curry combs belong in every tack room. Some pleasure-horse owners keep a few basic farrier tools such as a rasp and hoof-trimming knife. Sweat scrapers, sponges and rags are always needed.

Some horse owners have everything an equipment catalog offers. Others might use a stack of feed sacks for a saddle pad and tie their gear together with binding twine. No matter what the situation, every barn needs a jar of petroleum jelly. This miracle goo will soften manure matted in hair, perform numerous first-aid tasks, moisten dry, cracking leather or even loosen sluggish rusty metal joints in buckles or hinges.

The list of extras could go on and on. Every year manufacturers present innovative equipment for the horse enthusiast. There's a new horn cover to make a roper's dally grip better. New bit and saddle styles are developed and endorsed by trainers and performers. But the average horse owner can accumulate a few of the basics and greatly enjoy being or becoming a Western rider.

# Part III

# SHOWING THE WESTERN HORSE

# 9

# Advice for the Novice Western Rider

The challenge of taming a wild and spirited horse is a particularly appealing one to beginning horse enthusiasts. It is thrilling and romantic to dream of an inexperienced but determined hero melting the furious stallion into a giant mass of gentle tenderness. And it is a warm story in which a youngster acquires a lovable foal, and they grow and learn together until both are unbeatable champions on the show circuit. These two circumstances can take place safely and successfully only in the pages of a novel. Anyone new to the world of Western horses should begin at the beginning. He or she should never be embarrassed about any learning phase from ''This is a horse...'' to ''The winner is...'' Everybody in the saddle today had to learn how to stay there.

The vast majority of serious riding injuries are caused by unruly horses. A horse can be unruly for many reasons. He might be frightened, mishandled or just plain ornery. A prospective buyer must develop the ability to recognize and eliminate the possibility of such occurrences. This calls for careful scrutiny of horses' dispositions.

Disposition equals temperament plus personality. Horses rely heavily on basic instincts, and for this reason are often considered generally unpredictable. Such an assumption cannot be made wholesale. That would be unfair. Each one must be judged as an individual. Any horse will become frightened, jumpy or nervous at one time or another. Allowances must be made for his moods, strange surroundings, poor health or discomfort. But how a horse deals with these periods of stress is largely dependent upon his inherent disposition.

Some horses are born with wild or mean tendencies. When it is an inbred personality trait, kindness and patience will rarely settle the horse. This is not to say such horses should be treated harshly — *absolutely not*. But settling a horse and handling him are two different achievements. Many so-called outlaws can be made useful by patience and kindness and an experienced handler. But they will never be settled enough for a novice.

An older horse, at least over five years of age, makes an ideal beginner's mount. This animal will be wiser, let's hope, well trained, calm and patient with a learner. His personality is established, his temperament is evident, and his habits are formed. If the habits are good ones, he makes a willing companion. A progressive new rider will outgrow an extremely aged horse rapidly, but they often do make safe, dependable first horses.

The disadvantages of a young horse in inexperienced hands are endless. All his characteristics are being formed, and, if he is mishandled, will become permanent faults. Youngsters are easily spoiled, often jumpy and inclined to play. They quickly learn evasive measures such as rearing, bucking, running backwards, cow-kicking, threatening, etc. Every victory reinforces a habit. Strength, plenty of horse sense and experience are necessary to channel the youthful energies of a two- or three-year-old in the right direction. Seldom do two beginners make a safe or successful match.

A desirable Western horse is a solid, easygoing individual who acts well adjusted most of the time. He should not be a deadhead. Spirit and liveliness are not dangerous when easily controlled. A horse must be willing to place confidence in his rider and allow this trust to replace his fear instincts. He should, above all, be well trained and present a good temperament.

One of the first clues to the disposition of a horse is his eyes. If he has warm, friendly eyes, they probably accurately mirror his personality. If the eyes are quick, darting, suspicious and constantly displaying a large amount of white, he's likely to be a spooky, erratic animal. An occasional flash of white is no real danger signal, but a wild horse looks wild-eyed.

The only sure way to make an educated decision on a horse is get to know him. Any legitimate seller will be willing to allow a prospective buyer to ride the horse frequently under varying circumstances. Spend time with the horse. Work him until he's hot and tired. Observe him closely under stress and when he's relaxed. A really good horse is a necessity for a novice and a delightful luxury for anybody.

Following are the major attributes to be considered when looking for a reliable mount. The horse should be easily caught, both in the open and in a confined area. He should not turn his rump toward anyone approaching him or pin his ears back at them.

He should stand well when tied. He should permit necessary movement to go on around him and calmly accept it. Likewise, when free, the animal must be safe to be near. Some horses that would never kick or bite after being caught will charge across an acre field to attack.

He should willingly allow all four feet to be handled and not fight necessary brushing, combing, cleaning, saddling, etc.

It would be useful for the horse to be accustomed to a trailer or truck and to load and unload easily. He should ride with a minimum of fuss.

He should be still when a rider mounts, move well and easily into all gaits and calm down quickly after fast or strenuous work.

Good behavior around other horses is important, too. Some equine extroverts prefer being the only horse around. Consequently, they will kick, bite or threaten any horse within range.

A loudmouth squealer is more of an annoyance than a danger, but he draws much unwanted attention. An occasional whinny, nicker or murmur is to be expected, naturally. But some horses will scream as long as they think there's another one around to hear them.

Not the least valuable characteristic is a horse's size. If the rider is too little, the horse might actually forget he or she is up there. If the rider is too large, the horse will tire easily and balance poorly. Obviously, when a child rides a full-size horse, they will be out of proportion, but as close a match as possible is best.

The novice Western rider must strive to look like an equestrian. The goal for any polished rider is to operate a horse as an extension of his or her own body. This requires hours of riding and practicing the skills. Only when a rider becomes comfortable and relaxed in the proper posture will he or she appear to be accomplished. When a student is confident, sure-seated and ready, horse shows are the next grade level of education.

Horse shows offer the best opportunities for seeing how well horse and rider can work together. When the team is ready, competition is an impartial, objective teacher. Both horse and rider should be really

**This horse well illustrates being on the proper lead. Notice how he is allowing his forefoot that is on the inside of the turn to support and direct his weight. His body is barely curved and he is leaning slightly into the turn.** *Photo by Allen L. Bird, courtesy* Appaloosa News.

ready before good money is spent for the trip and entry fees. It is not at all unusual for a conscientious beginner, or even a seasoned rider with a green horse, to visit several horse shows before actually entering any classes. This familiarizes both with the hustle and bustle of showing, riding in an arena and mingling with other horses. After that, it is still best to begin in small shows and put more emphasis on gaining experience than winning ribbons.

Before you can even consider a show, the horse should take both leads well, back up, move easily into each gait and maintain it steadily and stand without fidgeting.

Always arrive at a show early, preferably one full day, if it is out of town. This gives horse and rider plenty of time to become accustomed to the arena, stall, and general area. The horse should have time to work in the ring before being judged. Playful horses need to be longed before they leave home and possibly again upon arrival at the show grounds. Brisk trotting will loosen up a tense horse. After a few snorts and deep breaths, he'll start relaxing and be ready to get down to business. Getting there early will prevent the nerve-shattering last-minute rush. Neither horse nor rider can overcome the upset of mad-dash preparation.

If the show requires staying overnight, make a complete checklist of what is needed. Know ahead of time which feeds will be available or if each exhibitor is to provide his or her own. Frequently, abrupt changes in diet will cause colic.

Know the rules of the show or approving association. Being aware of any special requirements will make the difference between a wasted trip and a good one. Some associations dictate how to hold the reins, what should be added to the basic tack (such as slicker, rope, etc.), whether a curb chain or a tie-down are allowed, and if a hackamore or bit is to be used.

What to wear is another question to be answered. Styles vary so throughout the country, there is no one mode of dress correct or incorrect. It is advantageous to look well groomed, neat and not frilly or gaudy. Overdressing reveals an amateur and doesn't encourage the

**Rosie Leola, a performance mare, is beautifully prepared for being shown. She is impeccably groomed and her attractive but not elaborate equipment complements her total appearance.**

proper kind of notice. Here again, associations have their individual requirements.

The rider isn't the only one who should look clean and sharp. A horse's appearance is important, too. His fetlocks, bridle gap and ears should be trimmed. (Don't completely remove hair from ears or fetlocks if the weather is extremely hot or cold. It protects from chill and insects and diverts running sweat from sensitive areas.) Whiskers should be cut off and any white areas should be washed. If the weather is mild, an entire bath with horse shampoo and thorough rinsing would make him gleam. Horses that may be shown with roached or trimmed manes and thinned tails should have it done just before the show. A few weeks' growth looks ragged. Others need their full manes and tails washed and combed.

Don't spring any surprises on a horse just before show time. He ought to be used to a truck or trailer. Don't expect him to make a good showing if the trip to it is his first one. Don't leave new equipment to be tried out on the big day, either. A bit especially should be introduced ahead of time to get both horse and rider accustomed to it.

A good impression is always formed of the contestant who practices good sportsmanship and common courtesy in the ring. Follow a safe distance behind the horse in front, and avoid riding between another exhibitor and the judge. Make every effort to keep up with the average speed of the gait asked for, and stay free of bunching up. Often a quick circle to find an opening on the rail is necessary and quite acceptable. Work on the rail, taking care not to cut corners or run down judges and ring stewards. Any horse who acts ugly toward other horses in the ring should be kept at home until his manners improve.

*Look* as if exhibiting a horse is fun. An unsmiling, frightened expression detracts from what might be an otherwise good-looking team. Persons who look miserable on their horses do not convey confidence, no matter how skillful they may actually be. Smile! The judge will take a closer look, if it's just to smile back.

More and more Western show horses today are registered. Officially transferred registration papers should be in the hands of the buyer before a sale is finalized. Many an unsuspecting buyer has paid a registered horse price only to receive word form the breed association that some requirement has been violated, nullifying the registration. And too, it seems fires are unusually prevalent among erstwhile horse traders offering registered stock: "Sure she's registered, but her papers got burned up in the fire last year."

Horse shows sanctioned by breed associations and excluding non-registered stock are increasing in numbers every year, all across the country. The growing popularity of owning registered animals has stiffened competition noticeably. Still, there are scores of excellent *grade* horses available. These are horses which are not purebred, and for any one of many reasons, not registerable in a breed association. If a prospective buyer does not intend to raise purebred stock or show in restricted events, registration papers are an added expense. For the owner who rides for pleasure and maybe takes in a few neighborhood shows each season, the price and dependability of a Western-type grade horse can't be beat.

# 10

# Western Performance Classes

Perhaps a designation between performance classes and working classes is not entirely accurate. Any time a horse is being shown and judged, he is working and performing, simultaneously. Horses trained for work or working classes are specialists. Their training is a sort of graduate work in a chosen field. But, no matter what classification titles are attributed to an exhibitor, the basics of horsemanship, time and hard work combine to produce the true performer.

## Halter Classes

The Western horse shown at halter must do more than look pretty and stand quietly. He is not just a happy accident, an animal that came into the world with a good conformation. Winning halter horses are made and maintained by constant superb care and daily work. Excellent condition and conformation are most important to a halter prospect, but proper training makes a display of these attributes possible. A judge will look and look again at a horse that stands well, handles easily, acts alert and moves well. If the raving beauty lined up next to him is slinging his head or stomping, the consideration will be brief and unfavorable.

Condition determines the success of a halter horse. Good conformation is simply a foundation upon which to build. A horse who has straight legs, a well-set head, a pleasing color, and is nicely proportioned is not automatically a born halter champion. In the final analysis, it is his overall condition that accents a superior build or compensates for a faulty one.

Diet plays the leading role in a horse's condition. While amounts and preferences vary with individuals, plenty of high-quality grain and hay is imperative. Nutritional supplements are extras well worth the effort and expense when developing an animal to his peak condition. Clean water and salt (in an above-ground container) should be available at all times.

**A picture of a winning halter horse is a picture of nearly perfect conformation and conditioning.** *Photo by Allen L. Bird, courtesy* **Appaloosa News.**

Regular worming and vaccinations are an integral part of a horse's physical fitness program. Any health problems call for immediate attention by a veterinarian.

Daily exercise is another requirement for the serious halter contender. This forms hard, powerful muscles out of what would otherwise be soft flab. The horse needs regular activity in all three gaits at varying speeds. If he is too young or not broken to ride, longe line work or ponying from another horse does well. This, as well as all other routine horse management tasks, offers the best results when performed on a strict schedule.

Adequate hoof care is another top-of-the-list priority. Corrective trimming and shoeing can do a lot to camouflage some of nature's quirks. Toeing in or out, forging, and some hock and leg shapes can be altered somewhat by a knowledgeable farrier. If a horse's feet and legs are well designed, it still requires good shoeing habits to keep them that way. Do not shoe a horse only a day or two before showing him. He is likely to be tenderfooted and won't do his best.

Only when a horse has attained his top physical condition can he truly compete in today's halter classes. Further preparation for showing a halter horse involves external maintenance. He is now in a position to look his best. Most show horses are kept in a stall and blanketed. This prevents scrapes, scratches, insect bites and sun bleaching. Vigorous brushing every day helps promote a clean, healthy coat.

A complete bath with livestock shampoo and thorough rinsing is best the day of the show. If that isn't possible, it should be given no earlier than the day before. Other show-day touch-ups include cleaning and clipping the ears, cutting whiskers off the muzzle and chin, trimming the mane, bridle gap, lower legs and fetlocks. Ringside is the final opportunity for readying a halter horse. Going over him with a towel takes off any dust brought to the surface by brushing. Use a damp cloth to wipe out eyes and nostrils. The last thing before walking into the arena should be a head-to-toe spraying with an insect-repellent coat-shine product. Also, some associations allow hoof-blacking and this should be late on the agenda.

While the halter horse's equipment is minimal, its impact is not. A well-fitting show halter is a must. Most exhibitors still prefer leather, but nylon ones are appearing more and more. Whichever a handler chooses, it should be clean, in good repair, and flattering to the horse's head. The lead should match the halter. A rope or nylon lead with a leather halter or vice versa is out of place.

The handler should, as always, be neat and properly

Western-attired. Many regulars in classes choose clothes to blend with their horse's color. Coordinated equipment adds an extra touch of completeness. Compatibility is eye-catching and attractive. Gaudiness is not.

Most association-sponsored shows divide their halter classes by horses' sex and age. It is imperative that the handler know exactly which class he or she qualifies for and when it will be called. Early arrivals at the gate have time for those last-minute extras that may mean the difference between winning and not. They also have a chance to relax, reassure themselves that they and their horses are just right for the all-important step into the ring. For, from that moment, they are being judged.

It is a wise exhibitor who carefully chooses his or her place in the group. A horse that contrasts sharply with the ones around it will get the judge's attention. This spotlight, of course, is to be avoided if it doesn't show the horse off to best advantage.

The handler needs to maintain a safe distance from the preceding horse, keep up with the pace, and stay alert for instructions from the judge. When asked to line up, leave a comfortable but not excessive distance between contestants. Each horse will be expected to stand quietly, squarely on his feet with head up and ears forward. The handler may move from side to side to avoid getting between the judge and the horse. If the horse shifts out of a proper stance, resetting his feet is permissible.

Patterns of work differ from show to show. So, when the ring steward gives instructions for the workout, be prompt and brisk. There is no need to rush—always take the time to do well. Each will be expected to walk and trot toward and away from the judge, make his turns smoothly and flatfooted and return to the lineup. Re-enter the line from the rear and set the horse back up. Judging continues until the entire class has been dismissed from the ring.

From some spectators' point of view, halter classes might not have much to offer. "A bunch of horses just standing there" does not involve the action and pageantry of many other Western classes. But to those who understand the training and fine points of horse care involved, the halter class represents top performers.


## Horsemanship or Equitation Classes

A fairly recent addition to the list of Western performance classes is Stock Seat Equitation or Western Horsemanship. Although such a specifically named class is still not present in all shows, its popularity is growing. A stock seat is the ideal way to sit a Western horse in any activity.

The rider's proper seat, hand position, leg position and balance are all necessary for the best action of the horse. He will be well balanced, able to execute smooth gait transitions, turn easily and stop well if his rider is consistently in the right place at the right time on his back.

Some classes of this type will allow each participant to work individually. Others display all entries at once. The horses will be asked to walk, jog and lope both ways in the ring, back easily and stand quietly. This must be done on a loose rein with as little detectable signaling from the rider as possible. The ability of the rider is the major judging consideration.

**Pam McNamara Scott illustrates a good Stock Seat Equitation seat. Here, Daddy's Dandy has carried her to the blue in Stock Seat Equitation. In 1972, Pam won the Leo Carrier Memorial Trophy, an honor bestowed yearly on an outstanding youth member of the Association. *Courtesy the Pinto Horse Association of America.***

The foundation of good equitation is the foot's position in the stirrup. Weight should be over the balls of the feet with heels below toes, which are pointing slightly outward. This shifts more of the support to the outside edge, thus putting the knees in the proper position. Correct foot placement transfers most of the grip to the thighs and makes a rider sit down deeply in the saddle. The descended heels reinforce this deep seat and place the calves closer to the horse for better control.

A rider needs to sit in a straight line with legs underneath, not thrust forward or drifting back. If an imaginary line were drawn down the side of an equitation rider, it would pass from the shoulder behind the knee and through the heel.

The body's position from the seat up is important, too. A straight back neither slumped nor arched, even shoulders and arms hanging relaxed but close to the sides are all aids to good balance. Reins are held through the hand, lightly but firmly a few inches ahead of the body and just high enough to clear the saddle horn.

Well-fitted, tailored clothes are the best choice for an equitation or horsemanship contestant. The rider should be impeccably dressed with tie and hat straight and every minor detail considered. The outfit should blend with the horse's coloring. In both looks and movement, horse and rider should appear as one. No other type of class in a Western horse show requires such striving for perfection.

## Western Pleasure Class

The Western Pleasure Class is easily the most popular class among exhibitors in a Western show. The entrants are judged on performance, conformation of the horse, and skill of the rider. The horses are shown at a walk, jog and lope with no undue restraint required during any gait or when changing gaits. These activities are done both ways in the ring, and horses are expected to take the correct lead in either direction. (When asked to change direction, horses are to be reversed away from the rail.) Most judges will ask the class to go directly from a lope to a quick standstill.

The Western pleasure horse must back easily and promptly upon a minimal signal from the rider.

Hackamores and popular bit bridles are allowed by most associations, and work-type stock saddles are preferred. All equipment is subject to inspection by the judge.

Seat and hands are the same as those of the equitation or horsemanship classes. The reins cannot change hands.

Suitable Western clothes are required, usually with spurs and chaps optional. Some associations suggest a coiled rope and a slicker be tied to the saddle.

Frequently, a judge will work larger classes in groups with the finalists of each group comprising the last workout. Or, the entire group will perform, and all but the finalists will be dismissed from the arena. Again, an exhibitor must remember that judging begins the moment the horse sets foot inside the ring and doesn't end until he's back outside.

Horse and rider should be true to the class's name. They should look as if the performance is a pleasure — for both of them.

## Trail Class

Trail classes are designed to exhibit horses' maneuverability and adaptability to unexpected situations which might occur on a wilderness trail or outdoor bridle path. A good trail horse is often called upon to protect his rider from such things as being scraped off by trees or falling into sink holes. He is called upon to cross through water as well as over it, see and accept foreign objects on the trail, and go over obstacles in the path when they can't be avoided.

Many encounters such as steep hills, picking a way through dense undergrowth and hour after hour of riding cannot be reproduced in an arena. At times, persons responsible for devising an arena course lose sight of a sensitive trail horse's ability to use common sense. In many cases, an obstacle is not sufficiently restrictive. For example, a bridge or gate in the middle of an open arena with nothing extending from either side indicates that the logical thing to do would be go around it. It is almost unreasonable to urge a horse over an object when he is only a step or two from avoiding it completely.

Of course, while he has his own decisions to make, a trail horse must be willing to listen to the rider, too. He must trust his handler enough to proceed upon repeated urging — if the request is reasonable. This is apparently the reasoning behind such obstacles as a bucket of fresh animal's blood, a burlap sack full of empty cans, and a trailer with a hog tied in one side. Obstructions as imaginative as this, however, are few.

Most trail classes contain a gate to be opened, passed through and closed, several logs to be stepped over in succession, and a wooden bridge. The rider is asked to put on and take off a slicker, carry an ordinary object from one place to another, back the horse through an L-shaped course, dismount and lead the horse over a small jump.

**A good trail horse will approach obstacles as this Appaloosa is doing. He is alert and attentive to where he is going, and carefully choosing his footing. Yet, he is confident and willing without undue urging from his rider. *Photo by Allen L. Bird, courtesy Appaloosa News.***

Some shows install a real or make-believe water hazard, require a horse to stay ground-tied while his rider walks away from him, and ask the handler to send the horse into a trailer.

All tasks must be completed with a minimum of balking on the horse's part, fumbling on the rider's part and upsetting the necessary structures. The gate obstacle may or may not be the entry gate to the ring. Exhibitors work the course one at a time, moving counterclockwise. There is usually a time limit set for completing the course.

Gaits between obstacles are chosen by the judge. Also, group rail work can be announced after each contestant has completed the course, individually.

Standard Western equipment and clothes are the rule. Associations differ on which extra items, such as a rope or slicker, should be tied to the saddle for a trail class.

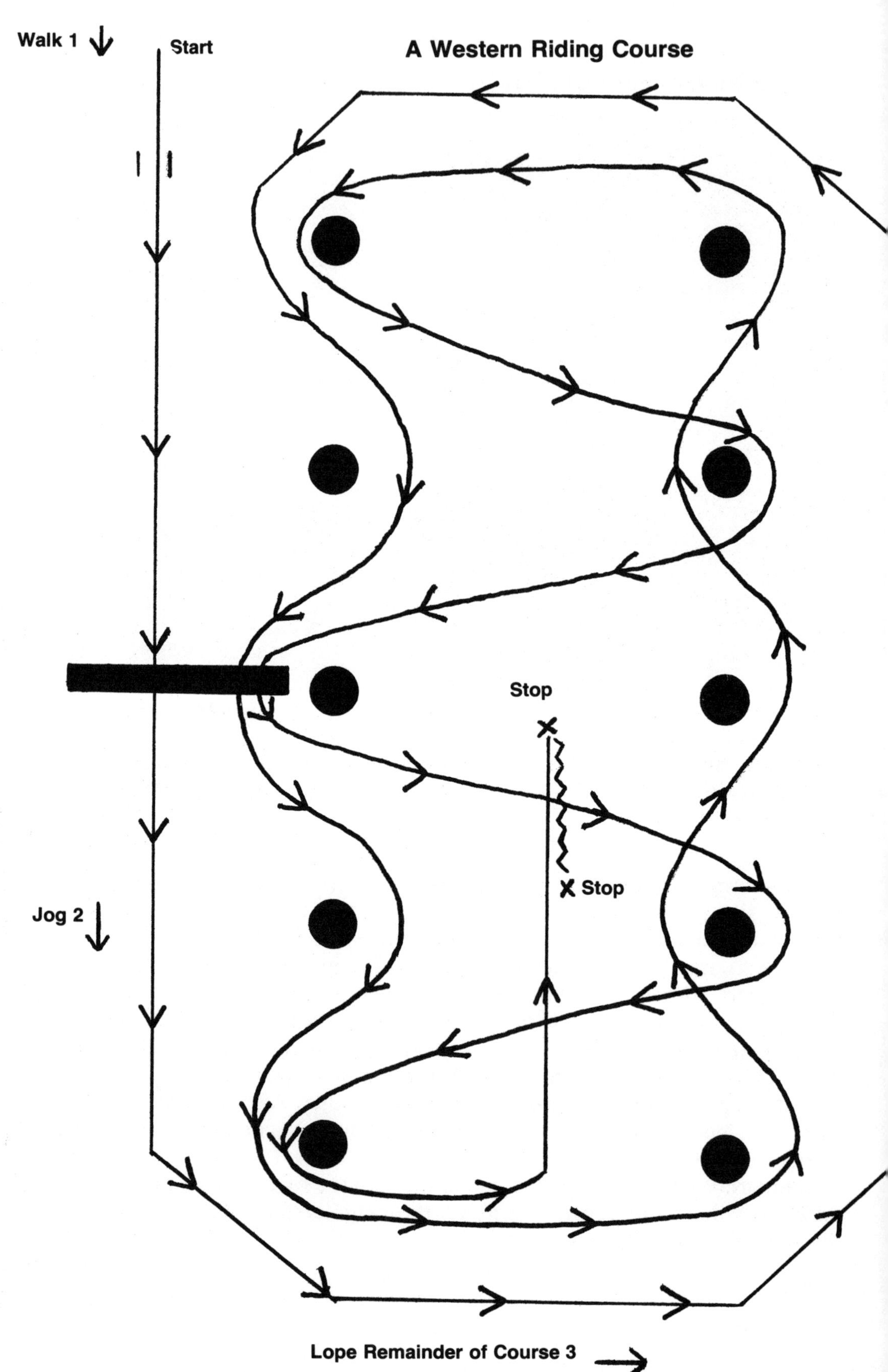

Walk 1
Start
A Western Riding Course
Stop
Stop
Jog 2
Lope Remainder of Course 3

Even the coolest mount will object at one time or another. Judges instantly respect an alert horse that approaches obstacles with curiosity and caution and gives them a long, hard look, then yields calmly to the insistence of his rider. A horse that will blunder through and across anything without so much as a second glance suggests ignorance or the rider's early knowledge of the course. A nervous, jumpy horse that actually shies from or steadfastly refuses obstacles is not yet an arena-ready trail horse. He probably needs to spend some more time out on trails — real ones!

## Western Riding

This is another class which is designed to judge horses' disposition, ease of moving and response to their riders. They are judged at a walk, jog, and lope. They are expected to change leads and give a well-mannered, comfortable ride around and through obstacles.

Standard Western clothes and equipment are required or encouraged. As before, the judge makes the final decision on the acceptability of a piece of equipment.

The most frequent pattern appearing in Western riding classes includes the following: A gate to be opened and closed by the rider; walking to and over an obstacle high enough to break the horse's stride; trotting several yards; moving into a lope and serpentine along two lines (one down each side of the arena) of barrels or poles. These should be placed approximately forty feet from each other in a straight line.

After weaving down one side and back the other, the rider should crisscross the arena, making a turn around every other standard. Each of these activities must include passing over the stride-breaking obstacle. When the final turn is made at the end of a line of standards, the horse runs to the center of the ring, stops and backs several feet. He should then stand quietly until dismissed.

Western Riding is another fairly recent newcomer to Western shows. It is an exciting class to participate in as well as to watch. It is a skillful, high-speed combination of trail-class knowledge and equitation riding.

# 11

# Western Working Classes

Western working classes developed, obviously, from ranch and cattle work. The sophistication of these classes has resulted in the creation of rules and regulations for the good of horse and rider. It has also produced highly skilled animals and trainers who delight thousands of spectators yearly.

Yesterday's cowboy didn't have time to polish his mount into the fine, brilliant performer of the seventies. Then and now it takes heart and cow sense in both horse and rider. Reining, roping, cutting and working cowhorse are the main work events for Western show horses. Each class depicts in an arena what cowboys have done for decades on the plains and ranches.

## Reining

The Western reining horse in action is a joy to behold. A well-trained reining horse appears to the observer to work by mental telepathy. It takes a well-trained rider to make it look that way.

Each breed association which endorses a reining class will recommend a specific reining pattern. Some associations have approved as many as five patterns. In any sanctioned show, the judge chooses one pattern, and all contestants perform it, each participant working individually. Getting off course is often immediate disqualification.

Requirements for the performance of reining horses are generally alike, even among the different breeds. The horse will be called upon to lope easily, run fast, stop, back, stand quietly for a few seconds, lope in small and large circles or figure eights, roll back right and left, pivot right and left and walk. Each rider is to stand before the judge for an inspection of horse and tack. The contestant is then dismissed from the ring.

The best working arena is at least 50 x 150 feet. This allows for the desired speed of straightaway running and uncrowded maneuvering.

While the fine points of judging differ from group to group and even judge to judge, the major faults of reining horses and riders can be generalized. When stopping, the horse should not bounce, step sideways or throw his head up. Refusal to change leads, knocking over pattern markers, clumsiness (stumbling), excessive mouth activity (jawing, open mouth), crooked backing, or signs of irritability (head-slinging, tail-wringing) will lower a contestant's rating. Also, judges do not look favorably upon a horse who anticipates the pattern. The purpose of the class is to exhibit overall training, not the fact that one pattern can be drilled into a horse's brain.

The rider will also drop his rating several points by violating basic Western horsemanship rules. Unnecessary roughness or overhandling (spurring, jerking, petting), holding to any portion of the saddle, losing a stirrup or changing hands on the reins are the most common mistakes.

Reining equipment includes general Western attire, a stock saddle and a reasonable bit or basic hackamore. Well-fitting, flat curb chains are usually permitted, but here, as in all Western events, they are subject to inspection by the judge.


## Roping

Calf- and steer-roping contests call for precision riding and split second timing on the parts of both horse and roper. In all roping events, Western attire is usually required and always recommended. Anything a judge considers severe may be prohibited, and any unnecessary action to induce a horse to perform better is considered a fault. Most roping events are governed by the rules of rodeo associations.

Any horse being judged must start from behind a regulation barrier. In some instances of team roping, one horse at a time is judged.

**Ernie Taylor, 1973 calf-roping champion, drops a loop while his horse is getting ready to go to work.** *Courtesy the Rodeo Cowboys Association, Inc.*

Otherwise, there are two judges, one for each team member. In roping contests, only the horse is judged. Of course, it is the cowboy's responsibility to qualify by dropping a loop on a calf or steer, but the points are made by the horse. Judging begins with a horse's behavior behind the barrier and ends when the run is completed.

In the calf-roping event, there is no team, just a single roper. The horse is judged on the following: willingness to remain behind the barrier until the calf crosses a scoring line and his speed to the calf after breaking the barrier (scoring); his ability to maintain a desirable roping position relative to the calf (rating); his stop; his attention to the calf and holding a firm, straight rope (working the rope); and his manners as the roper returns and remounts him.

A roper has a two-minute time limit in which to throw two loops, if needed. When the contestant plans to throw a second loop in case he misses the first, it must be already made in a second rope tied to his saddle. If he carries one rope and misses, he is disqualified. He is not allowed to build a new loop.

When a roper gets his calf, he steps out of the saddle to make the tie and the horse is on his own. A good roping horse will watch the calf closely and keep the rope taut and straight. If the cowboy has to throw the calf, his horse must take up any slack created but not drag the calf. The calf's feet must be tied securely enough for him to be unable to stand or free his feet for a designated number of seconds. The roper's time stops when he indicates the tie has been made. If the calf remains immobile for the allotted time, the roper's time and the horse's score stand. The best score in the least amount of time is the object. Exceeding the two-minute time period is disqualifying.

Steer roping is done in teams consisting of a heading horse and a heeling horse. The heading horse is responsible for rating the steer, slowing him down and setting him in the proper position for the heeler's rope. The heeling horse must follow easily, maintain the proper position, jerk the steer off his feet and keep him accessible for the header to tie.

They, too, have only two minutes from the time the steer charges from his chute. A header must drop his loop around both horns or the neck. A heeler must catch one or both hind legs. The horse being judged is restricted to two loops, like the calf roper. There are some events which allow the rider *not* being judged to make and throw as many loops as are necessary (within the time limit). Still other team events require a roper to carry only one rope and recoil if a second loop is thrown.

In some contests, the steer must be tied in the area above the heels and below the hocks. The header carries the pigging string (short length of rope for tying a calf's or steer's legs) and does the tying.

In dally-roping, the steer is not tied. When both catches have been made, the ropers remain mounted and when both horses face the steer stretched between them, the run is completed.


## Cutting

Cutting cattle has moved from a day-to-day job to a skillful sport for many Westerners. Show rings abound with everyone from the weekend cutter to the highly trained professional. But good cutting horses take time — lots of it, experience and brains. "Good" means not necessarily a champion, but a well-trained, responsive, eager cowhorse.

Any number of reasons necessitated a working cowboy's separating a single animal from the herd and preventing its return. This called for a horse whose natural ability and learned skill can be excelled by none.

Leo Camarillo, 1973 team roping champion in action. *Courtesy the Rodeo Cowboys Association, Inc.*

The cutting horse is wisely thought of as the most highly trained Western horse in the world. While the real cutting horse contest is between the horse and the cow worked, it is the spirit of competition that brings hundreds of cutting horse riders and enthusiasts together every year.

The herd from which individuals are to be worked has approximately twenty head of young cattle and is kept at one end of the arena by herd holders. The contestant has two and one-half minutes to work two or three cows. An excellent performance on two head is better than a mediocre performance on three.

The horse may approach the herd at any speed, but must ease into it quietly without disturbing the cows. He should show no hesitation or reluctance to approach the herd. Neither should he display any ill-tempered aggression toward the animals. The true cutting horse can wander about slowly, deep in the herd until a cow has been chosen. He moves, always alert and concentrating, at the direction of his rider as they proceed to remove the cow from the herd.

When the cow is outside the herd, the rider gives the horse his head and lets him take over. Reining by the rider from this point is penalizing.

Two mounted riders stationed near the center of the arena act as turn-back men. They keep the calf facing the horse and the herd. The successful cutting horse must jump quicker, dash faster, run harder and sometimes even stare longer than the determined cow who wants badly to rejoin his buddies. But the horse must never overreact and pass up the cow. They often work nose to nose, with the horse's uncanny power to second-guess the cow coming out on top—most of the time.

After several seconds of a good workout, the rider reins the horse away from that cow and re-enters the herd to select another. A contestant will receive a poor score if he quits the cow when the horse appears to be losing control of it, or if the cow is advancing on the horse. Again, the horse must calmly move through the herd until another cow is singled out and he can go back to work.

The cutting horse is judged on his ability to drive a cow, circulate in the herd without scattering it, perform with no cue or reining from his rider while keeping a cow out of the herd. His score will also depend upon how hard the cow made him work and generally how he handled himself in all situations.

## Working Cowhorse

This event combines reining education and cow sense. Each contestant is required to run a designated reining pattern and work a cow. In some shows, the reining is completed by all entries, one at a time, before the cattle work begins. In others, each completes both phases before leaving the arena.

The reining portion involves running, sliding to a stop, backing and turning, all in a designated sequence. The horse should be quick, smooth, well on his feet at all times and sharply responsive to a light rein.

For the cattle-working portion of the class, a single cow is turned into the arena. The contestant holds it at one end of the ring for a reasonable length of time to indicate the horse is watching it. The cow is then allowed to run down the ring side. The horse must turn it twice in each direction against the fence. Finally, the participant moves the cow to the center of the arena and circles it once to the right and once to the left. A judge has the option of requesting additional work.

Each breed association which promotes a Working Cowhorse class will stipulate requirements in its rule book. Generally, Western wear is desired and a coiled rope is tied to the saddle. In some shows, there are special Hackamore Working Cowhorse classes, but as a rule, regular stock equipment is used.

When in action, the cowhorse should be alert and attentive. He shouldn't rush or anticipate. He should work willingly and easily, exhibiting the qualities of an all-around working ranch animal.

# 12

# Gymkhana — Games on Horseback

The word "gymkhana" means a series of athletic contests, especially racing. It is an appropriate word when applied to the games on horseback that are a growing part of many Western horse shows. The race is against time, and the horses are athletes in every sense of the word.

Gymkhana horses are often unjustly overlooked in discussions of thorough training, good manners and skill. They are fast, supple, maneuverable, responsive, energetic and highly trained animals. They have to be. Only a game horse will explode into a dead run from a standstill, zigzag through poles or turn around barrels — all at top speed. Only a game horse would dash the length of an arena then settle down and wait for his rider to get off him and do something weird like crawl through a barrel.

A good gymkhana mount needs hot blood and a cool head. A winning gymkhana mount needs endless hours of training and practice. He must stay in top physical condition, because he is accustomed to giving all he's got to every performance. He may not be a registered horse. He may not even have a gorgeous conformation. But he has the heart and the guts and the will to be a dedicated member of a precision athletic team.

The number of games to be played on horseback is limitless. Following are a few of the favorites. Even each game can have several variations, but the ones seen most frequently are described.

Except when otherwise stated, all the games are run against the clock. Western equipment and dress are required in most large shows.


## Barrel Racing

Barrel racing has almost been removed from the realm of a game, but it is a gymkhana event. Many riders, the majority of them female, have pursued it professionally. The Cowgirls' Barrel Race has become a standard money-winning event in most rodeo performances.

Barrel racing as we know it today probably drifted across the land from Texas oildrum country. Some idle cowhand set up a triangle of barrels and proceeded to see how fast Ol' Paint could get around them.

The starting line is approximately 25 yards before the first two barrels. The rider can cross the starting line at a run. The clock begins when the horse's nose crosses the starting line. The rider may choose whether to begin his or her run with the left or right barrel. Whichever it is, the horse must pass the barrel, make a 360 degree turn around it and move to the second barrel, approximately 35 yards across the arena from the first. Another 360 degree turn and on to the barrel at the triangle's point, some 40 yards down the arena from the first two. After a full turn around barrel number three, the team deadheads back to the starting line. The clock stops when the horse's nose crosses it again.

The contestant completing the course in the shortest time is the winner. In case of a tie, there is a run-off. Some associations require the winner to run within two seconds of the original ride time, or have another run-off.

Groups vary on the penalties to be imposed on barrel racers. Some say a knocked-over barrel is disqualifying. Others add five or ten seconds to the contestant's time. If a rider bumps a barrel, it doesn't make any difference. But if it tips enough to be righted by the racer's hand, there is a penalty incurred. Some declare it a disqualification, others add seconds to the time.

The cowhand might have gotten the idea for his barrel course from the Indians. It is believed they located tree stumps in a symmetrical arrangement and raced each other around them.

Today, some associations sponsor what is called a Stump Race. For this event, two barrel courses similar to the one previously described are set up in the arena. Two contestants compete at once. After each

**Close — but not too close — turns are the secrets of champion barrel racers. In Barrel Races or Stump Races, the running horses are true athletes.** *Photo by Allen L. Bird, courtesy* **Appaloosa News.**

# Barrel Racing Course

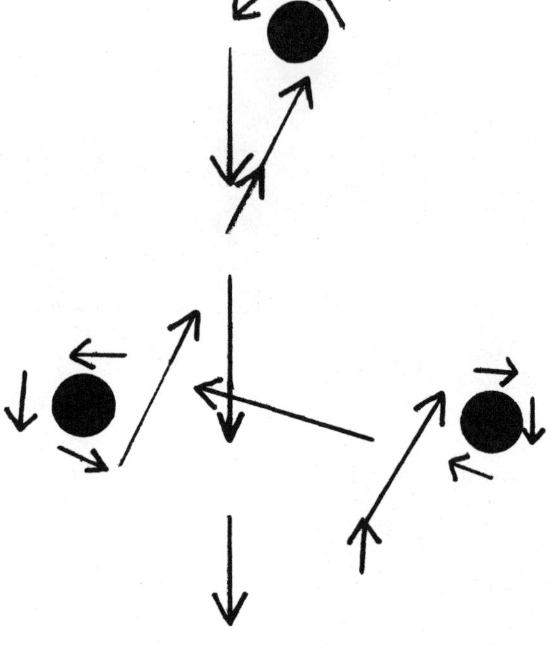



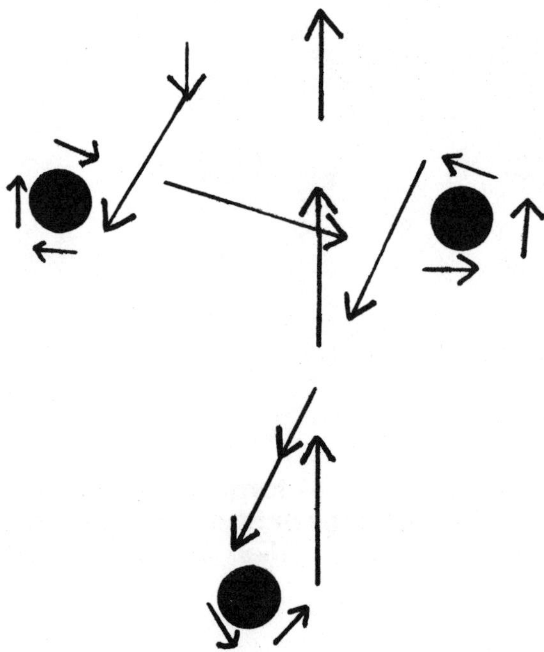

## Stump Race — Two Courses Combined

pair has run once, the winners of the first go-round begin the run-offs. The final winner is an exhausted but happy victor.


## Boot Race

Each contestant places his or her left boot in a pile at one end of the arena. A starting line is designated at the opposite end and all riders are mounted behind it. At a signal, they race to the pile, dismount, pick out their own boots, put them on, remount and race back across the finish line. The first one back *wearing matched boots* is the winner.

Some groups will increase the difficulty by requiring both boots to be left in the jumble. The first one to the pile has by far the biggest job!


## Flat Race

This race is run hundreds of times a year in back yards or open fields just to prove one horse can outrun another. A playday or gymkhana sponsoring a flat race must have at least minimum regulations.

If there is no track available, a specific distance should be clearly defined. There must also be enough room beyond the finish line to permit runners to stop safely.

Contestants draw for positions and gather behind a starting line. At the signal, they are off and running. Since such races are usually limited to six or eight horses, several heats may be necessary. The winners of the heats then compete in a final race.


## Flag Race

This game involves moving flags from one place to another or exchanging them. The course can be set up with three barrels in a triangle, much like the barrel race. On the first and third barrels will be a gallon bucket of sand with a flag stuck in it. The flags must be of different colors and the sticks should be about 18 inches long.

It is approximately 30 yards from the starting line to the first flag, and the contestant's time begins when the horse's nose crosses it. The racer carries one flag, runs to the first barrel and exchanges flags, runs around barrel number two and on to the third. Here, he or she jabs the flag being carried into this bucket, grabs the one already there and heads for home! The time stops when they cross the line with a flag in hand.

If a group prefers to run against each other instead of the clock, the course can be arranged differently. Place two barrels or buckets containing one flag each at the far end of the arena. Two riders, running at the same time, race across the starting line, pick up a flag on their way around the barrel, and the first one back across the line with a flag is the winner.


## Keyhole Race

This is an interesting race against time because the rider has to be a little careful. A blundering, mad dash will gain nothing in this race but disqualification.

A course the shape of a keyhole is laid out with lime or some other white powder substance. The alley should be at least 10 feet long and 4 feet wide. The turning circle should be 20-25 feet in diameter.

A contestant runs across the starting line and the time begins. The horse must run down the alley, into the circle, turn around and run back out the alley — without stepping on the white line at any point. The horse that can execute a rollback in the circle is less likely to kick up a telltale white cloud of dust!


## Pole Bending

Pole bending, one of the most frequently run gymkhana events, is second only to barrel racing in popularity. It requires not only speed, but the all-around Western skills such as reining, changing leads, quick stopping and the rollback.

The number of poles used and the distance between them varies from show to show. There are usually six to eight poles set approximately 20 feet apart in a straight line. The poles have a heavy base and are set on top of the ground. They should stand upright, but must be reasonably easy to tip over.

The contestant races across the starting line, down the straightaway to the last pole. The rider turns around it and weaves in and out of each pole. He or she then makes a complete turn around the other end pole, weaves *back* through them and runs for the finish line. Which side to begin the run on is usually the rider's option.

Again, two sets of poles can be set up to accommodate those riders who prefer heat races against each other to those against a stopwatch.

# Keyhole Race

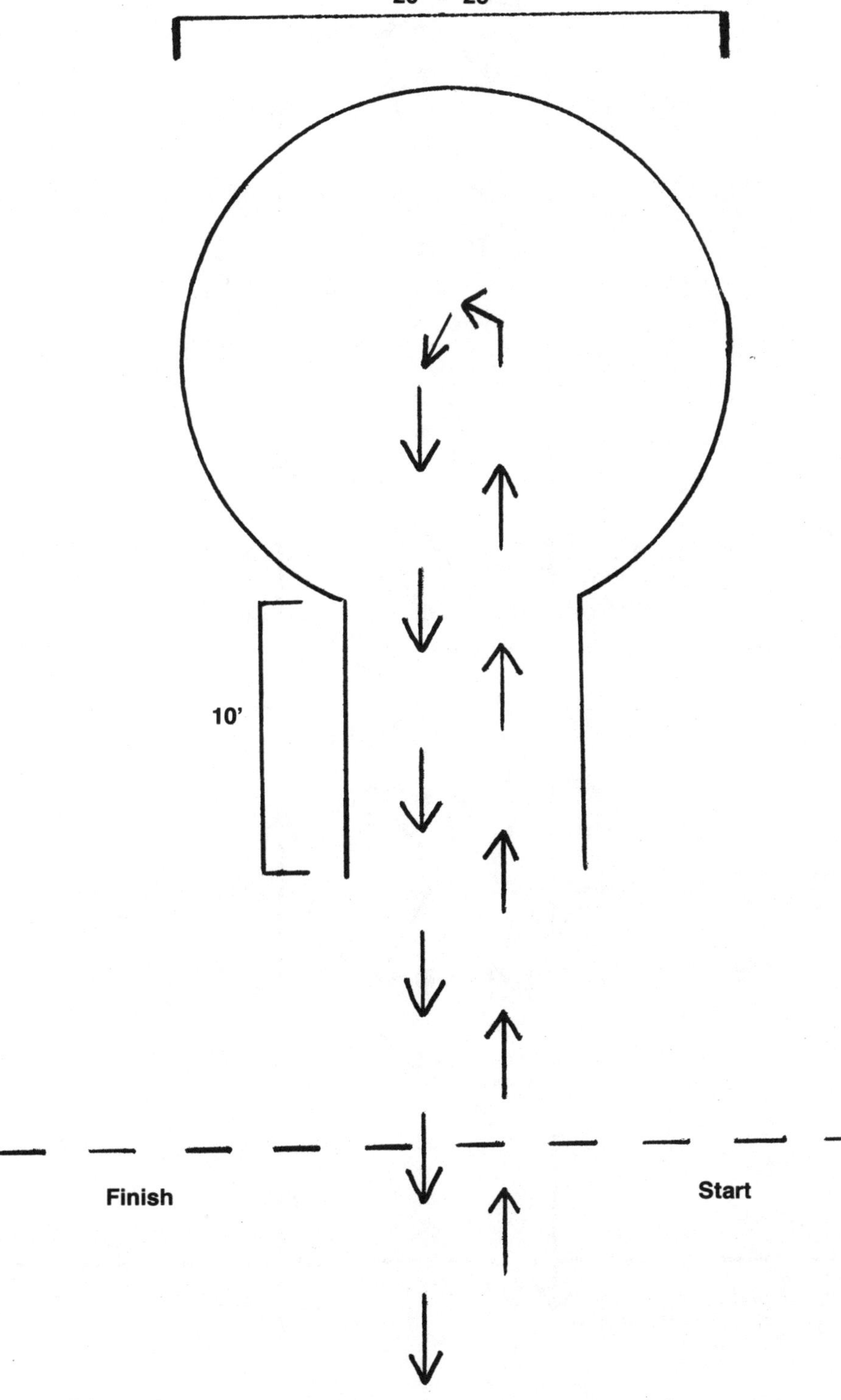

# Pole Bending

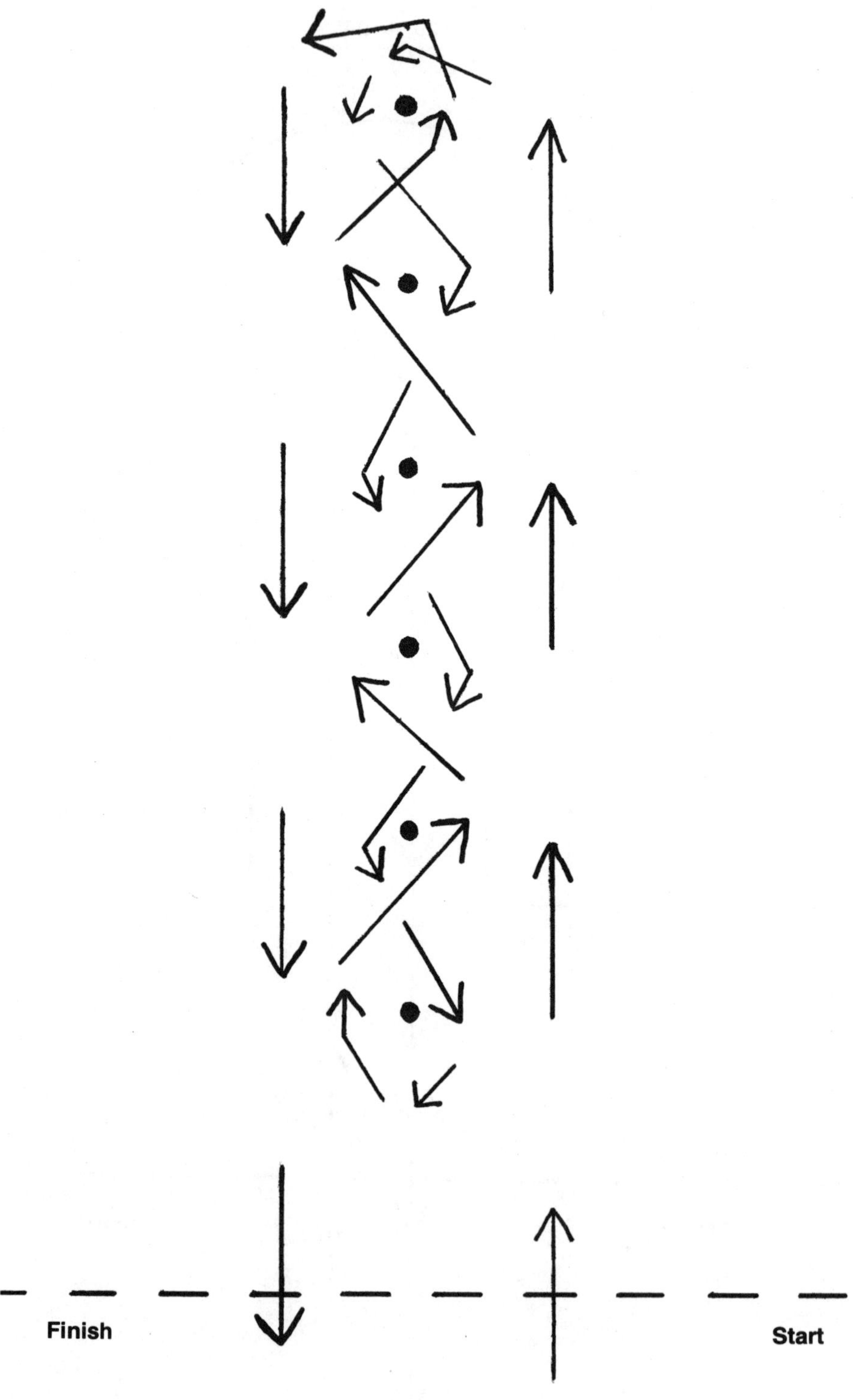

## Pony Express Race

The origin of this old-time relay race is as obvious in its name as in the way it is conducted. It is usually run over a mile distance. A team is comprised of four riders stationed a quarter mile apart. The first rider must mount, carry an object (baton, saddle bag, etc.) to rider number two, dismount and pass it to him or her. This rider repeats the action to number three, three to four, and number four races across the finish line with the object.

## Potato Race

This is another race which has as many variations as there are organizers.

One popular course uses the three-barrel triangle. The first barrel holds a box of potatoes or is constructed with a rim high enough to hold several potatoes. A rider crosses the starting line, runs to the first barrel and, on the way around it, grabs a potato. The contestant then runs to and around the second barrel and passes barrel number three which is open-ended and throws in the spud.

A surprising number of potatoes hit the top edge of the barrel. If a judge decides the biggest chunk fell into the barrel, the rider qualifies. If the larger piece fell to the outside, or the contestant missed the opening altogether, he or she is out of the running.

## Rescue Race

The rescue race is another crowd pleaser which probably started life as a real necessity. Anybody who found himself afoot amid a bunch of running horses would probably grab onto the first familiar saddle going by and hitch a ride. The clock is the pursuing enemy today, but contestants are just as determined as if there were real danger.

This event calls for a pair of riders. One waits at the far end of the arena in a marked circle or behind a barrel. The mounted rider races across the starting line and down the arena. As the horse turns to run back, the waiting team member swings (or is pulled) up behind the rider. They must cross the finish line riding double.

Some shows rule that once the rescued person's feet leave the ground, they cannot touch down again. Others allow them to hit the ground several times between the pickup point and the finish line.

Whatever the rule, too much or too little "jump" can miss the rumble seat entirely and land both team members out of the winnings.


## Rope Race

This is a scramble race which is a thrill to watch and a bruiser to run. A cable is stretched across the arena several feet above the head of a mounted adult rider. On this cable are ropes secured to metal rings which slide freely on the cable. The ends of the ropes can be reached by mounted riders. There is one less rope than there are participants.

All contestants gather at the end of the arena opposite the cable. At a starting sound, they all race to the ropes and try to grab one. The real challenge is not getting a rope, it's holding on to it! A rider not only has to get the horse to stop at exactly the right place and time, but needs to get there before somebody jerks the cable and sets the ropes dancing wildly.

In each run, one rider is eliminated and one rope removed. It is not unusual to see a rider hang on to a rope at the expense of losing his or her horse. This is disqualifying, however, and the dangler must surrender the rope to the remaining mounted rider. (Unless, of course, he can swing there long enough for his horse to walk back under him!)

Obviously, the last run — with two riders and one rope — is a collision course to an exciting finish.


## Tunnel Race

Here is a timed event calling for a large barrel or small people. A barrel with both ends open is placed at the far end of the arena. The contestant races to the barrel, dismounts, tips it over, crawls through and, if his horse is still around, remounts and hurries back across the finish line. Many a tunnel racer discovers just how important ground tying really is — during the long walk back to the starting gate!

## 13

# Rodeo, an American Tradition

The quiet Sunday afternoon in the latter half of the 1800s, a brawny cowpoke licked his cigarette paper, slid it through his fingers, crimped one end and taunted his partner, "See that bull over there..." The bet was on. And nearly as fast the cowboy was off — off the indignant bull, that is.

From just such an obscure beginning, rodeo has bucked, stomped and snorted its way off the plains and out of the corrals across America, into Canada and now all over the world. The stakes have risen from "If I stay on him eight seconds, you buy a round next Saturday night," to several million dollars yearly.

A rodeo performance is a wild and woolly conglomeration of color, excitement, noise, music, danger, skill and fun. It is a spectacle often labeled cruel and inhuman to animals and men. But a little consideration will reveal every rodeo event, with the exception of bull or steer riding and barrel racing, was a necessary function on a working cattle outfit. Broncs *had* to be busted. Cattle *had* to be roped, thrown, tied and branded, and this often required wrestling the critter to the ground.

Out of the chute for a wild ride! Saddle bronc riding is a rodeo event straight out of the pages of American history. *Courtesy the Rodeo Cowboys Association, Inc.*

The earlier days of rodeo may have seen mistreatment or abuse to animals. But for over twenty years the Rodeo Cowboys Association has followed strict rules to prevent injury to contracted livestock. They have their own inspection forces and work closely with the American Humane Association. It has been estimated that the average death and injury percentages of farm and ranch animals is twice that of rodeo animals.

Actually, rodeos take greater measures to protect their stock than do most other groups working with animals. Rodeo horses or bulls work eight or ten seconds a week and spend the rest of the time eating and sleeping. They get the best food and are not restricted to stalls year

**Riding vicious bulls was not routine during early cattle days, but it is a challenge few competition cowboys can resist. A Brahma bull is the meanest, most dangerous animal a rodeo contestant can ride.** *Courtesy the Rodeo Cowboys Association, Inc.*

round. They rest in pastures during the off season and get immediate veterinary attention when needed.

Bucking animals, except for the bulls that are just plain mean, are usually not vicious. Stock contractors tour the country as ''talent scouts'' looking for the roughest broncs they can find. The star of the chutes next season might be a gentle, hardworking farm horse who decided to change his lifestyle. Or, it may be the all-time favorite ''outlaw that could never be ridden.'' Whatever the situation, bucking horses are not crazy. They are smart — and lazy. They have no intention of working for a living and will fight anybody who tries to make them do so.

Of course, a bronc's personality can work in reverse. A real rip-snorter who has pitched cowboys for years may suddenly decide to retire. Some afternoon in front of thousands of people, he'll trot out of his chute without so much as a hump in his back and never buck again. An estimated one out of twenty broncs bought by a promoter will remain a dependable rogue. For this reason alone, cowboys make every effort to keep the animals happy, healthy and full of buck. In fact, cowboys think so highly of good bucking horses, they vote for a Bucking Horse of the Year every season and induct the all-time greats into the Bucking Horse Hall of Fame.

**The bronc and the rider give each other undivided attention before the chute gate opens.** *Courtesy the Rodeo Cowboys Association, Inc.*

Casual observers often develop misconceptions about the equipment used in rodeos. Any equipment could be altered and used to hurt a horse, steer, bull or calf. But regulated rodeos would never tolerate misuse of equipment. The animals' well-being is higher on the priority list than the cowboys'!

True bucking horses are born to buck, not aggravated into it. The flank strap does not hurt them or *make* them buck; they buck to get that thing off their backs. The strap simply makes a good bronc better. It makes him kick higher and longer. A horse who doesn't want to buck, won't no matter how he's strapped.

It is not uncommon for a rider to pet and talk to the bronc as he settles onto his back in the chute. This relaxes him, makes him more aware of the rider, and he'll buck better.

The sheepskin-covered leather strap is equipped with a quick release catch. After a cowboy has made his ride or hit the dirt, a pickup man grabs the strap's loose end and one yank loosens or removes it. This is more a courtesy than a necessity. It is done to prevent the animal's overtiring himself. Many broncs will stop kicking after they've unloaded their cargo, anyway.

Spurs are another offender to some spectators. There are carefully enforced rules governing their use, and the infrequent cuts are regrett-

**Branding time in the Old West gave us Steer Wrestling. There is no iron waiting for this fellow, but he is still about to hit the dust!** *Courtesy the Rodeo Cowboys Association, Inc.*

able accidents which receive immediate attention. The rowel, or points, of spurs are dull and must rotate freely. They give the cowboy one of the few advantages he's allowed by offering him a little more grip. He can't just hang on with his spurs, though. Rules require constant movement of his heels. Experienced riders know an animal in pain is discouraged and won't buck. Contesting cowboys certainly don't want that to happen — ever.

Steer wrestling and roping come in for their share of criticism, too. But medical studies indicate a cow's muscular structure is tough enough to safely withstand the jerk or twisting involved. There is usually thick wrapping at the base of their horns to prevent rope irritation. These animals, too, are worked for brief periods with long rests in between. A cowboy cannot make a decent showing on tired, sore or lethargic cattle.

Rodeo is one sport in which the adversaries are rarely evenly matched. Contestants have few advantages, and the animals have almost everything in their favor. But that's the way it is supposed to be. To equalize the proportions by maintaining unhealthy, injured or

**Take away the crowd, the arena and 75 or 80 years, and this cowboy would just be doing his job on a roundup. With his pigging string clinched in his teeth and a good, solid loop on the calf, he could have him branded in short order. But since this little one already wears a brand, they are working for money and points. *Courtesy the Rodeo Cowboys Association, Inc.***

**Joe Alexander exhibiting what made him 1973 Bareback Bronc Riding champ. Getting with a bronc's movements is essential to a high-scoring ride.** *Courtesy the Rodeo Cowboys Association, Inc.*

poorly kept stock would be a cruelty no professional would condone. Only an animal in top condition can make a top performance and produce top winners. A cowboy is only as good as the animals he uses, and being the best is what it's all about.

Rodeo is the only professional sport which requires its contestants to pay to participate. Entry fees range from around $25 to $100 and up, depending on the type of show. Each cowboy is assigned a number and every head of livestock is numbered, also. The cowboys draw from the livestock numbers to determine who rides what. No cowboy rides, ropes or wrestles the same animal twice.

In the riding events, stock and cowboys both are judged on their respective performances in the allotted time. The animals are rated 65 to 85 on how hard the ride was, and the rider is given from 1 to 20 points for how well he rode. A hard ride is one in which the bull or bronc kicks high, bucks wildly, does a lot of twisting and turning and keeps at it until the rider is off his back. An animal is marked down for bucking straightaway or running. For a good ride, a cowboy must bound out of the chute with his spurs forward of the animal's shoulder. His form, spurring action and how long he's aboard determine what rating he receives. If he doesn't stay on the full time (8 to 10 seconds), he's disqualified.

Public rodeo performances usually run three hours and include comedy acts, trick riders and ropers or singers in addition to the actual competition. Therefore, some go-rounds are held during other hours. This allows more point accumulation action than is available during the show. It also prevents the stock from being exhausted.

A competitor gets one point for every dollar he wins in a year. So it is necessary for a contestant with his eye on a championship to travel to as many rodeos as possible during the year. It isn't unusual for an ambitious cowboy to fly around to several shows a week during the peak season. He'll need rigs and horses, if he doesn't have time to carry around his own. He might even need entry-fee money, if he's had a run of bad luck. And there's always another cowboy ready to lend him all three.

True sportsmanship abounds in the world of rodeo. Cowboys will advise each other on an animal they've experienced — how it moves, the best way to hold on, what to expect, etc. Everybody pulls his weight at the chutes and in the catch pens. Everybody hates an injury and regrets a bad ride. The competition is keen, but the brotherhood is keener.

**14**

# Rodeo's Main Events

**Bareback Bronc Riding**

If there weren't still cowboys around who think they can ride a wild, outlaw horse better than anyone else, the bareback riding event would have been put out to pasture long ago. But the challenge of riding eight seconds of a whirling mass of equine fury continues to draw hardy, adventuresome athletes into rodeo arenas.

Today's bareback rider comes out a bone-fracturing second to the horse in advantages. With no saddle, all there is to hold is a handle sewn to a leather strap which is cinched around the horse's middle. The rider can grasp the handle with one hand only, and he must not touch the horse or any part of himself with his free hand. If he does — even accidentally — he is disqualified.

The cowboy eases onto the bronc's back in a narrow chute. When he's on well, with his heels ready, he'll give the word. His time and judging begin the instant the chute gate is opened. On the first jump out, his spurs must be in front of the horse's shoulders. He will make a better ride if he can get a good ''lick'' (spurring rhythm) going with the horse's movements. Naturally, the longer he stays on, the more chance he'll have to get with his horse. This in turn increases his likelihood of completing the ride.

At the end of eight seconds, a horn or whistle blows, and the cowboy is either already walking out of the arena or looking for the best way to get off so he can. There are two mounted riders, called pickup men, nearby to help him off and jerk the horse's flank strap loose. Whichever pickup man is closest when the time is up rides alongside, lets the cowboy grab his shoulders or the saddle and pull himself off the bronc. If the bucking horse moves away, the cowboy can safely drop to the ground. If not, he'll cling to the pickup man or get behind his saddle and stay until the flying hoofs are gone.

The bronc is herded into the holding area, his job finished and flank strap removed. If he rode the full time, the cowboy waits to hear his score. If he didn't, he thinks long and hard about what he'll do differently next time.

A re-ride can be awarded if the animal doesn't provide a scoring ride the first time out. When a bronc or bull won't buck, knocks the rider off balance coming out of the chute, deliberately throws himself or falls to the ground, the cowboy draws another stock number. His re-ride usually comes at the end of that particular event or during one of the go-rounds not open to the public.


## Bull Riding

Rodeo's toughest challenge is riding a Brahma bull. Not all bulls ridden are Brahmas, but they make up a large portion of the bucking bull population. Any bull who can be as mean and cantankerous as a Brahma is welcome on any rodeo string. A fierce bull is the one animal that would be as happy to grind the cowboy to a pulp as he is to get the little creature off him.

These huge animals are good at hurting a cowboy before he gets thrown. There have been many fractured faces from the erratic slinging of a bull's head. An animal with a reputation for this trick usually gets some of the length sawed off his lethal horns.

A cowboy's anchor on this ride is a flat braided rope looped around the bull's middle. There cannot be any wraps or knots to keep it on him. The cow bell hung under the bull's brisket has two purposes. The main one is its weight pulls the rope loose upon the cowboy's departure. Second, until it falls completely off, it reminds everybody there's a bull loose.

There is a holding loop attached to or braided into the rope. A rider inserts his gloved hand into the loop, palm up, and a helper standing on the chute pulls the slack out of the rope. He then passes the free end

**Bobby Stiner, 1973 Bull Riding champion, is riding high! Note how tightly Bobby's hand is bound under its strap. Note also the shortened, dull horns on the cavorting critter.** *Courtesy the Rodeo Cowboys Association, Inc.*

across his palm, once behind his knuckles and across his palm again. Both glove and rope have resin on them, and the rider is squeezing with all he's got when he nods his readiness. The gate springs open and another cowboy rides a dirty, gray hurricane to a face full of dust or a pocket full of prize money.

The ride is an eight-second eternity, and the free hand must stay clear of the bull at all times. At the end of the ride, the cowboy must have a portion of the rope left in his holding hand. The bull rider doesn't have to spur for points, but it helps him stay on.

The worst part of bull riding comes when the ride is over. There is only one way off, and it's the same at the end of eight seconds as it is any other time — jump or fall. Pickup men can't be used, because bulls will charge and gore a horse as quickly as they will a man. Here is where the rodeo clown earns his pay.

This cowboy with a big, red nose dressed up in funny clothes may have a few routines to amuse the audience. But his real job comes during the bull-riding event. He must be in exactly the right place at the right time to divert the bull's attention from the fallen cowboy. Sometimes it is a simple matter of running across the bull's line of vision while the rider scrambles to safety. Other times, if the animal is really after the rider, the clown will have to make a closer pass, slap the bull on the nose or shove the cowboy out of the way.

The worst danger of all is the rider's getting hung up in the rigging. Often a cowboy's hand is bound so tightly, he can neither free it from the handhold nor slip his hand out of the glove. He must have immediate help or he'll be tossed about like a yo-yo. Literally, bull-riding cowboys' lives depend upon the function of a rodeo clown.

Bull riders have one rather dubious advantage over horse-riding contestants. They are less likely to draw a dud. Bulls are more consistently rank than horses.


## Saddle Bronc Riding

In the days of the Old West, range-bred horses were seldom brought in for riding until they were four or five years old. Bronc busters used to travel around the country breaking horses to the saddle for a price per head. When horse breaking moved to the realm of slow, patient gentling and training, bronc busting moved to the rodeo.

The saddle is about half help, half hazard. The rider does have stirrups to aid his balance and help absorb the shocks. But if he loses one, he is disqualified. The saddle usually has the horn sawed off, but in the case of a fall, it's still harder than the horse's fleshy back. A saddle also offers more opportunities to get dangerously entangled.

Saddle broncs are ridden with a halter and one rope rein. This rein is used only for balance, it is useless in controlling a horse. Horses buck with their heads down, some farther than others. Where a cowboy holds the rein is most important to his balance. It can make the difference between falling off backwards, getting yanked off over the horse's head, or making a good ride.

A saddle does the cowboy another favor (?). It adds two seconds to his ride! He still can't touch the horse or equipment with his free hand, and he should be spurring every step of the way. He can't change hands on the rein, and he can't wrap the rein around his hand. At the end of the ride, if he is fortunate enough to have endured the ten seconds, the cowboy is rescued by the pickup men. The bronc's flank strap is released and he's led or driven out of the arena.

**Bill Smith, 1973 Saddle Bronc champion, drew a high kicker! The free arm is held up and well away from the body to keep from accidentally touching himself or the horse with it.** *Courtesy the Rodeo Cowboys Association, Inc.*

## Steer Wrestling

This event is one of the many which had its origin in the early ranch days. No one knows how many range hands were forced to wrestle a balky steer to the ground for branding, doctoring or any other reason. However, the origin of the steer-wrestling arena performance as we know it is attributed to Bill Pickett, a black cowboy.

Bill had the reputation of being one of the roughest, toughest, best cowhands on the famed 101 Ranch. Tradition has it that Bill got so mad when a stubborn bull refused to enter a corral, he jumped five or six feet from his saddle onto the bull's neck. Grabbing one horn in each hand, he twisted the bull's head around, clutched its upper lip in his teeth "like a bulldog," and dragged it to the ground. Pickett's "bull-dogging" got such wide acclaim, he began doing it regularly. And other

**How a steer wrestler's horse breaks away from him has much to do with his position for bringing down the steer. Here Bob Marshall, 1973 Steer Wrestling Champion, made a quick catch and is ready to hit the ground.** *Courtesy the Rodeo Cowboys Association, Inc.*

cowboys, being nature's most ardent competitors, had to get into the act.

Biting into the animal's lip remained, for the most part, a Pickett trademark. The name Steer Wrestling has gradually replaced Bulldogging on rodeo programs, but participating cowboys are still 'doggers.

Steer-wrestling cowboys must furnish their own horse. They must also make arrangements for a *hazer*. The hazer is a mounted rider who keeps the steer running straight, once the animal leaves the chute. The success of a cowboy's ride frequently depends upon the ability of his hazer, for a wild running steer can ruin a contestant's chances to qualify.

The steer-wrestling horse is an important, highly trained specialist. His riders trust him to know what to do and to do it. He is often shorter than most rodeo horses, with stocky, powerful legs and heavily muscled shoulders.

Two of the three participants start from behind a barrier. The steer stands behind a gate, the 'dogger is in a stall-like structure on the steer's left, and the hazer is on its right. A rope barrier with an easily breakable connection is stretched in front of the 'dogger's horse. While the animal is in the chute, a rope the length of the steer's head start (which is determined by the length of the arena) is tied to its horns. This also has a weak connection such as light twine. When the 'dogger signals readiness, the steer's gate is opened, its rope pulls a pin which breaks the 'dogger's barrier, and he bounds out after the steer. A contestant gets ten seconds added to his time if his horse breaks the barrier before the steer releases it.

The cowboy attempts to overtake the steer, yet maintain a few feet between it and himself. When alongside at precisely the right distance, he leans down, reaches for the horns and begins easing out of the saddle. Twisting the steer's head actually begins at this point, before the rider is completely off his horse. Next, the horse veers away from the steer's path. The precision with which he makes this move will affect how the 'dogger's feet hit the ground. He must land with heels digging into the arena floor. Only with good stopping action can he bring the steer to a halt.

After the steer is under control, the cowboy continues pulling its head to swing the hindquarters around. The 'dogger then moves a hand from one horn to the steer's nose and gives the final twist that drops the steer on its side. It must fall flat on its left side, with all four feet free. If the steer falls on the wrong side it is an elimination.

Since this is a timed event, a fast, accurate team is every steer wrestler's goal.

## Roping

Steer and calf roping are two more popular championship contests. Since these events also appear in other Western shows besides rodeos, they are detailed in Chapter 11.

## Girls' Barrel Race

In the early days of rodeo, a few women competed in the main events. Today, there is a Girls' Rodeo Association which produces its own rodeos and coordinates women's activities in others.

The girls' barrel race is present in professional rodeos throughout the country. Its course is three barrels to be run in a cloverleaf pattern. Distances between barrels and from starting line to first barrel are determined by the size of the arena. It is a race against the clock, and the cowgirls are allowed a running start. Each has the option of taking either the right or left barrel first. A knocked over barrel is a disqualification.

There are championships awarded yearly to the leading barrel racer. The skills of professional cowgirls and their horses are highly developed and add much to any performance.

## Rodeo Contests

True to American rodeo's nature, its contests are more rugged and dangerous than any others in the horse world. Most of these are races with the winner being the first to complete the specific requirements. With no points or championships, the prize is usually the "pot," or the combined entry fees of all participants in each contest. Here again, the phenomenon called a cowboy pays for the privilege of getting rope-burned, knocked down and cow-tromped.

One of the favorites of excitable spectators and daredevil cowboys is the Wild Horse Race. Fifteen or twenty unbroken and unwilling wild horses are turned loose at one end of the arena. A team can be either two or three cowboys.

At the starting signal, all teams rush into the kicking, snorting, biting, striking herd of hell-on-the-hoof. The main goal is to stay alive. The object of the contest is to ride one of these outlaws back across the starting line.

One team member ropes a horse, the other one or two put a saddle and halter on him — somehow — and one rides him back. These broncs are pitching, spinning proof that a flank strap doesn't squeeze the buck out of a horse! The winning team is the one whose member got his mount aimed at the finish line and stuck with him until he vaulted over it. Horses win, too. Some break free and gallop away, leaving a battered team to drag halter, saddle or each other back across the arena.

Another crowd-pleasing free-for-all is the Wild Cow Milking Contest. In this one, cows gather at one end of the arena with an equal number of ropers at the other. The same number of cowboys, each with a small-necked bottle, wait in an appointed area.

At a starting signal, the ropers run for the cows, attempt to rope and hold them while the dust-covered dairymaids try to milk their pop bottles full.

These aren't tame cows some area farmer has loaned. Not an Ol' Bossy in the herd will stand and chew her cud. She's wild and she's mad at both ends — the rope and the rough-handed cowboy.

In some wild cow milking contests, the winner is the first one across the finish line with the most milk in his bottle. In others, the cowboys are given a certain length of time for milking. At a time's-up signal, the bottle containing the most milk is declared winner.

A third major rodeo contest is straight out of the old trail-driving days. It is a death-courting scramble of horseflesh requiring nearly every skill known in cowboydom. It is the Chuck Wagon Race.

A racing unit consists of a chuck wagon pulled by four horses, one driver and two outriders. This contest requires a race track or an equally large area.

Each unit gathers in the track's center field. The driver is in his place with one outrider at the rear of the wagon, poised and ready to throw the camp gear onto its tray. Crouched over the huge box, hands resting on it, he holds his horse's reins in his teeth. The other outrider is in front holding the team and his mount.

A starter sounds and the spectator is thrust into the world's fastest break-camp-pack-up-and-get-out-of-here, but with a few extra rules, just for fun.

The gear is hurled onto the tray and secured. The two outriders mount as the wagon explodes into the first maneuver. It must be driven in a figure eight around two barrels in the center of the track. The unit then heads for the straightaway (if it survives the melee in the center) and races a designated distance to the finish line. The gear box must remain intact, and both outriders must cross the finish line within 50 feet of the wagon's tail end or suffer a time penalty.

# TIPS FOR WESTERN HORSEMEN

**15**

# Tips on Early Handling

Since it would take volumes to thoroughly instruct owners in how to train their horses, Part IV lists, as simply as possible, some main objectives and how to achieve them. It includes specific hints and ideas the average Western rider may or may not be aware of. It is not intended to be a training course. Chapters 15-18 offer a comprehensive foundation or framework from which to pursue more technical, in-depth direction.

Persons successfully handling a foal must have a clear understanding of what he is. Naturally, he will grow into a 1,000-pounder who, for everyone's sake, had better be meek and well trained by the time he does. But until then, he is a baby — a silly, curious, energetic and wildly playful baby.

A young foal can be considered in several comparative areas similar to human toddlers. His attention span is short while his curiosity level is high and constant. He is first brave and daring, then reluctant and fearful. He is emotionally unstable and inclined to behave according to whims. Constant care and attention is needed to keep him happy, healthy, safe and growing into the adult he should be.

TIP *Look at everything in a foal's environment as a potential hazard.*

Here is a youngster who is extremely curious, but well behaved. Notice the firm, heavy muscles already appearing in the shoulders and hindquarters. This is the result of regular, frequent exercise. *Photo by Allen L. Bird, courtesy* Appaloosa News.

It is. Colts and fillies have an uncanny ability to get into trouble where none existed before. They are going to play, alone or with other horses, no matter where they are. They will run, kick and jump in a stall as well as in a pasture. The stall walls should be solidly built with no spaces between boards. Check for protruding nails or other sharp objects. Feed and water containers should be soft plastic and, for extra safety, removable.

Wiring, light fixtures, switches, water spigots and latches must all be out of a foal's reach — he has the most talented nose in the world! An enclosure with a low roof or beams is dangerous. Horses have been killed instantly by rearing and hitting the tops of their skulls against a solid object.

TIP *First halters should be heavy-duty, in good repair and correctly fitted.*

Even the smallest foals are strong enough to give handlers a run for their money. They are extremely impulsive and a firm grip with dependable equipment is the only restraint.

TIP *If at all practicable, load and transport a foal while it is still beside its mother.*

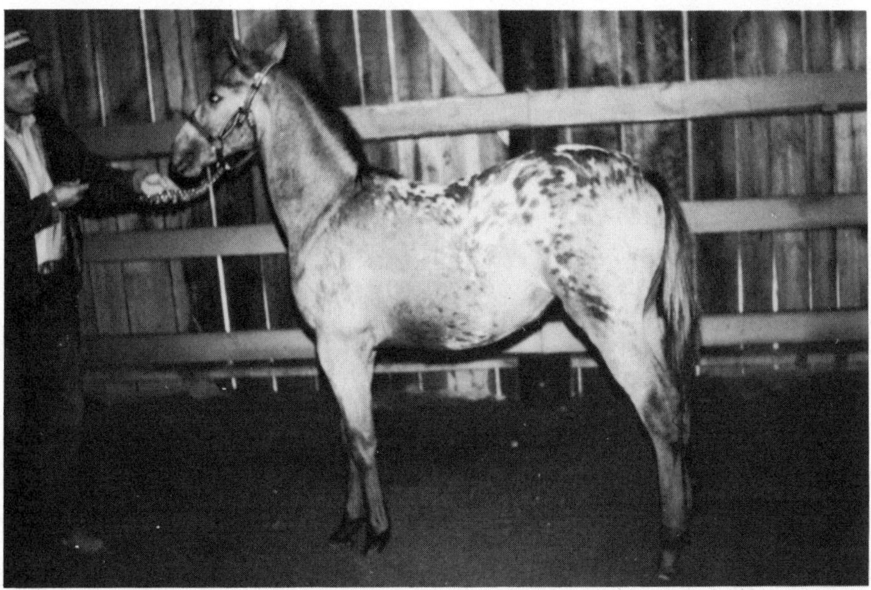

**A good, firm hold on a youngster is necessary to transmit instructions. Here, this filly's ears indicate she has divided her attention between trainer Earl Burchett and some activity behind her. She is half Appaloosa, half Thoroughbred, owned by Hidden Hills Farms.**

A calm, quiet, seasoned traveler is the easiest example for a young horse to follow. If the mare loads easily and rides comfortably, the little one will do the same.

TIP *The area where the foal is handled should be as danger-free as his constant surroundings.*

He just might get loose. A fear-crazed foal will run through fences and into all kinds of injurious objects. An area containing dangerous terrain, one near a highway or one with other animals which could compound the problem is not a wise place to halter-train a colt or filly.

TIP *Be gentle, consistent and patient when handling a foal.*

A young horse that learns early to fear people will never make the calm, gentle, tractable mount he could otherwise become. Love, trust, respect and confidence in his handler will make him work harder and learn faster.

TIP *Prevent as many mistakes as possible.*

Painful or frightening punishment does not remind a foal he has done wrong. It reinforces the dread of contact with people.

TIP *When leading, hold the foal's halter securely under his chin with the right hand and the lead in the left.*

If he gets bouncy or wants to lunge ahead, the handler can turn him in circles. This breaks his stride, and when he finds out his bolting trick won't get him anywhere but around in circles, he'll give it up. Be careful not to pull or push his head, though. He should be made to walk with his head and body straight.

TIP *Don't work with a horse under two years of age more than 30 minutes to one hour a day.*

He'll get tired and stop listening. Any effort to get a point across to a foal who is finished cooperating is an exasperating waste of time for both. Regular handling for brief periods will offer much better results than cram sessions.

TIP *When teaching a foal to stand tied, be sure of three main points.* (1) *Be certain what he is tied to will hold him.* Nothing will defeat the purpose of a tying lesson like a foal's ability to haul back on the rope and jerk it loose or uproot whatever is holding it. (2) *Tie him with a slip or safety knot.* Since he'll probably be standing there awhile, he needs to be able to get free in case he got into really bad trouble. Getting away is a bad idea, but a broken neck is worse. (3) *Tie him high and short.* Rope injuries are a leading cause of pain and discomfort, if not permanent lameness. If the foal has to eat while he's tied, leave him just enough rope to do so easily. Five or six feet of rope tied close to the ground is, at worst, a potential killer; at best, a sure accident. Simply stepping over the rope and lifting his head could touch off a thrashing chain reaction which would turn him every way but loose.

TIP *Spend plenty of time handling his head, face, ears and feet.*

This is where most of the work goes on and where most of his shyness will develop. A sack or blanket rubbed over his head and entire body is useful in gentling a young horse. It also prepares him for saddling and bridling.

He must learn to have all four feet lifted and held without fighting. He'll spend most of his life with shoes on, and ordinary hoof care should not be a life-and death struggle.

TIP *The first time a young horse is saddled, leave it on him for several hours.*

He won't like it, but if it's not cinched too tightly and is well padded, it won't hurt him. The more he becomes accustomed to it, the less he'll resent having it on.

TIP *Leading a green horse from another one often helps settle the trainee.*

An older, experienced mount is an example and a reassurance. The younger horse will get used to moving around with gear on him and stirrups bumping him.

TIP *Begin riding in a fenced area and use the corners.*

Turning instructions and the all-important ''whoa'' become instantly clear to a horse who has no alternative but to follow the instructions. To a bewildered horse with a fence on one side and his face in another, it would seem logical to respond to the signals and move out. No sane horse is going to keep running past a stop signal and a sharp ''whoa!'' when there is nowhere left to go.

TIP *Use all the signals early in a horse's training.*

When first breaking a horse, he'll respond only to direct reining (one rein in each hand). But as the right rein pulls his head to the right, the left rein should lie against the left side of his neck. This introduces neck reining. Leg pressure should accompany every hand signal.

TIP *Trot a lot.*

This gait is a relaxer and a muscle builder. It also teaches a young horse to obey signals at more speed than a walk, but does not encourage rambunctiousness as loping does.

TIP *After a horse is under control, ride on trails or in pastures part of each training session.*

A horse's experience is broadened and his tolerance is expanded when he is ridden in unfamiliar territory. He will be less jumpy if he is exposed to sights and sounds different from his stall and work area.

TIP *Do not shoe a young horse for his early training.*

Sensitive feet will keep his mind on where he's going. His feet shouldn't be sore, overworked or bruised, but shoes cover up an extra little bit of feeling which helps keep him well on the ground and concentrating.

TIP *Remember, backing is thoroughly foreign to a horse's nature. Be satisfied with two or three steps at first.*

Walking backwards is unnatural, and some horses require more persuasion than others to try. A light but insistent seesawing with the reins plus significant leg pressure will usually move a horse back. If the rider eagerly accepts a few steps while the horse is getting used to backing, the young student is less likely to resist.

TIP *Never ride into a barn.*

Unless a barn is a gigantic building with halls designed for riding, a mounted rider should never enter it. There are too many accident possibilities. Horses learn quickly when work is over and it's chow time. If they are ridden back to their stalls regularly, it becomes inviting to knock off a little early and head for home, whether the rider is ready or not.

TIP *The barn is home, sweet home – but not too sweet.*

A young horse is less likely to become sour if he has more work to do when he goes in. Ending a work session by giving him a quick brush-off and turning him into a stall to a gallon of grain and sweet, fresh hay makes it all too appealing. It's no wonder he wants to go back in after he's walked less than 30 feet away. Lead him into the barn, leave him saddled and tie him. Clean out his feet or work around him awhile. Then unsaddle, brush him, and finally, feed him. The barn won't be such an enticement if it is not an immediate reward.

Training a horse is a most demanding, time-consuming endeavor. Making a foal acceptable to society requires infinite patience and persistence. But the effort involved is rewarded manyfold when a trainer can see his or her green, balky youngster turn into a knowledgeable, willing worker.

# 16

# Tips for Working Horses — Reining, Roping, and Wrangling

Early ranches allowed their horses to run wild until full maturity. After the horses reached about five years of age, the cowboys would round them up, throw a saddle on each one, and ride the buck out of them. A horse was ''broke'' when a cowboy could rope, saddle and mount him — alone — and live to tell about it. These green horses didn't spend weeks in careful training. Their knowledge was gained firsthand. As soon as riders could stay on them, they went out on the range to do their jobs.

Compared to ranch working animals, show horses are pampered performers. They work every day on the same thing and then exhibit their skills for a few minutes in the show ring. But the ranch horse might have to work four or five hours after he's dog-tired. He has to be an all-around horse who's willing to perform his tasks over rocks, hills, ditches, holes; through brush and briars; in rain, sleet or snow. No sand or gravel composition flooring for him! And his show is never called off because of inclement weather.

**Although modern conveniences lighten a range horse's work load, he is still needed. Here, Quarter Horses are making a living the same way their sires and grandsires did.** *Courtesy the American Quarter Horse Association.*

A ranch cutting horse would probably be thrown out of a show. He dispenses with the fancy footwork because he's likely to have over 200 cattle to work. He just walks into the herd, moves out the cow his rider indicates and, with as little activity as possible, keeps them separated. Often, the cows he cuts out will have calves at their sides. This doubles the horse's work load.

The ranch horse's response is to the job to be done rather than to an intricate system of signals and cues. A poor rider is unlikely to ruin a settled working horse. Quite the contrary. A wise ranch animal is far more likely to change the rider. Many a greenhorn cowboy has been taught the fine points of range work by a competent horse.

A good all-around using horse is one who can change jobs if he's needed somewhere else. Although he might cut cattle for a living, he'll become a roping horse if his rider decides to rope off him. Chances are the roper's no champion, so the horse needn't be either. By the third or fourth missed loop, the ranch horse brings into action his major virtue — patience. Whenever the cowboy ropes his cow, Ol' Paint will be ready.

With the advent of helicopters and pickup trucks, vast cattle operations do not depend upon horses as they once did. They still remain a valuable part of the cattle industry, however, and a few basic points and preparations can make the difference between a good worker and a goof-off.

TIP *A young horse should not be expected to run fast and stop quick.*

His size simply can't handle it. His muscle structure and adolescent clumsiness won't allow him the strength and coordination necessary for bursts of speed and hard stops. He will probably be at least three years old before he is able to work at such a pace.

TIP *Introduce a young working horse to the rope early.*

The ideal time is the beginning of his training while he is becoming accustomed to everything else. The mounted rider should slowly and carefully pass a coiled rope up and down the horse's neck, around his ears and across his sides and rump. A loose end punching an eye or startling him will be a setback.

After the youngster has become accustomed to a rope being moved around him, the trainer can then make a loop and drop it gently, straight down to the ground beside him. Retrieve it cautiously, recoil it and drop it again. When the horse accepts this, progress methodically to twirling the rope slightly and, finally, swinging and throwing it.

TIP *Use a roping dummy.*

A bale of hay, a stump or a simulated steer is an excellent aid in schooling a horse who will be called upon to rope. It teaches him to approach objects head-on and confidently.

TIP *Expect a horse to blow sky high if he's really frightened.*

It is a basic instinct. When he is startled and faced with a situation he can't handle, he won't change his mind for a mere mortal. The best way to prevent frequent explosions is to provide the horse with as many varied situations as possible. While he is experiencing new sights, sounds and smells, he is also gaining confidence in human beings. After all, it was a human who saw him through all those spooky things!

TIP *Teach a using horse to ground-tie.*

A horse who will stand securely with his reins simply dropped to the ground will be an asset in countless situations. Since tying by the reins is a bad idea anyway, the dependably ground-tied horse is a relief to a working cowboy.

TIP *Logging is good practice for horses, whether or not they are destined to be ropers.*

Dragging a log or other heavy object from the saddle horn

familiarizes a horse with an unusual pressure on the saddle. It should not be too heavy, requiring undue exertion, but it should put a noticeable tug on the saddle.

Logging also accustoms a horse to having a commotion behind him and having his legs and sides touched while he is moving. Rustling leaves or leg-grabbing underbrush will be more easily tolerated by a horse whose early training included logging.

TIP *Ride a future roping horse behind a goat or slow-moving calf.*

When several hours are spent following another animal around, the horse gets the idea firmly in his head. Soon, he'll begin following on his own, watching the cattle and listening to his rider, all at the same time.

TIP *When herding horses, remember they are not as willing as cattle to bunch.*

If a horse herd is being moved into an enclosure, don't crowd them. Horses are apt to kick or bite in such circumstances, or sustain a hip or leg injury on a rail or gate post.

TIP *Hang a bell on the leader of a horse herd or the leader of each band.*

This will give the horse wrangler a head start on locating the bands after a whole night for scattering.

TIP *Horse wranglers, listen to your mount.*

When you are looking for other horses, he can probably start in the right direction before the bells are heard or the horses become visible. Your mount knows when his buddies are in the area. He can be depended upon to give many other helpful hints to a cowboy willing to listen to him.

# 17

# The Making of a Good Western Pleasure Horse

*Webster's Dictionary* defines pleasure as "agreeable sensation or emotion; amusement; what the will prefers." Add to that the unmistakable characteristics of a Western-type horse, and the term Western pleasure horse is easily understood. The true pleasure horse possesses agreeable emotions. He is the most popular mount for sheer amusement than any other in the horse world. He is ready and willing at the slightest indication to do what his rider's will prefers.

Everything involved in riding a Western pleasure horse should be a pleasure to both horse and rider. A well-trained, reliable pleasure horse is a comfortable animal that gives a comfortable ride. His way of going is completely natural but ground-covering. His jog is an easy one which the rider can sit without standing or posting and which the horse can maintain for hours on end. He performs constantly on a light rein, thus relieving his mouth of pain and pressure. The well-turned Western pleasure horse will do more for his rider with less handling and effort than any other horse in the world.

Spanish riding habits were the mold for our Western riding, not only in equipment, but in the movement and handling of the horse. They were lovers of fine gaits and easy motion, but they were dedicated to achieving all maneuvers on a loose rein. The horse that required tight reins and much handling was considered a spoiled horse.

A superb Western pleasure horse is no accident. He is not molded into a pleasure mount because he can't learn to do anything else. Many performance horses are too high-strung to be pleasure horses. Many halter champions do not have an adequate way of going to be considered pleasurable to ride. A genuine pleasure horse prospect is a relatively rare animal. Utmost care should be taken to preserve, encourage and magnify the elusive traits of a stately, respectable Western pleasure horse.

TIP *Early, gentle, confidence-building handling is the best insurance for developing a pleasure horse.*

A colt or filly's impression of the human animal comes early and is a lasting one. The sooner a young horse is happy and relaxed around people, the better. It gives him that much more practice in trusting.

TIP *If possible, handle a youngster frequently as an infant and a weanling, then turn him out for several months before starting intensive training.*

After he has had a little more time to grow up, he will be mature enough to adapt to more rigorous work programs. Even if he is brought back in at sixteen months to two years of age, he'll still remember people are not his enemies.

TIP *Prevent bad habits when possible. Discourage those already in existence.*

Pet a horse primarily around his neck or shoulders. It is a welcome reward. But petting around his head or face is likely to make him a head slinger.

If a horse is encouraged with feed, offer it to him from a pan or bucket. Constant hand feeding or tucking carrots in a pocket for the horse to nose out is cute. But he'll end up an annoying nibbler or a dangerous biter.

Too-long lessons or work sessions make a young horse tired and restless. He'll mess up or get himself in real trouble, and he's more likely to remember the bad happenings than the good. Training itself should be a pleasure.

TIP *A young horse is usually not inclined to attempt impossible tasks.*

Training should be undertaken with several things totally impossible. For instance, handling should begin where the little one can't possibly get away. He should be bitted in an apparatus he can't get off or get tangled in. He should be ridden first by someone he can't dislodge. Early successes at misbehavior will delay the gentling process so necessary to a pleasure horse.

This works two ways. If a trainer tries to force a young horse to do something he considers — at his age — impossible, he'll think the handler is crazy. An adequate training program involves keeping the animal's respect along with his confidence.

TIP *Allow a young horse to carry his head and neck at will for approximately the first year of riding.*

After he can handle himself and has achieved good balance with the bit and a rider, his flexion can be more easily modified, if desired.

TIP *Be sure a horse knows how to do what you are asking him to do.*

If he honestly does not understand, forcing the issue is useless and harmful to the relationship. A sensitive trainer can tell the difference between a truly bewildered youngster and one who's deliberately trying to get out of work.

TIP *Horses, like most animals, learn from each other.*

It is invaluable experience for a trainee to accompany a proficient older Western pleasure horse on many rides. He'll learn much by watching the pro move calmly and quietly through his gaits.

TIP *If a Western pleasure horse is bound for the show ring, continue to expose him to frequent trail or pasture riding.*

A horse that is bone-tired of going round and round in an arena will be a listless plodder. The variety of trail riding expands a horse's education, freshens his outlook and quickens his senses. If he is used to watching where he is going and what's happening around him, he will remain alert and attentive.

TIP *School a Western pleasure show horse in patterns unlike those he'll be asked to do in the ring.*

Here again, the trainer is trying to avoid monotony. Horses learn quickly to anticipate what is to come next in an arena performance. Some even become conditioned to announcers' voices. To please judge and spectator, the Western pleasure horse must always be controlled — easily but definitely — by the rider.

TIP *A trainer's horse is a tell-all mirror.*

An unrelenting, unreasonable, ill-tempered handler will produce a horse with the same personality. A person without the patience and time to ease a horse into the role of pleasure mount has no business attempting it.

TIP *If one training attitude can be considered more important than others, it is consistency.*

A horse who never knows what to expect from his handler will be edgy and constantly trying to outguess him or her. An animal as well as a trainer will have bad days. It is better to forego a poor lesson than to risk flared tempers and frightening confrontations. A firm hand and consistent, good-natured treatment will produce a steady, dependable Western pleasure horse every time.

# 18

# Common Horse Vices and Possible Cures

Bad habits in horses can range from a petty annoyance to a serious danger — to the horse or his handler. A saddening number of horses lose their lives because of vices they couldn't overcome and their owners couldn't eliminate. Injury and death can often be prevented by owners who are willing to become familiar with horse vices and what causes them. Whether a horse is a family pet or a ranch hand, he deserves the best of care and protection from himself if he develops a threatening pastime.

Boredom is the number one cause of horses' developing vices. To a healthy, energetic horse, those four walls of a box stall soon become a prison. The ideal situation would be to pasture all horses. But since this is impossible for countless reasons, the next best thing is to provide amusement and recreation for the confined horse.

Regular, frequent, vigorous exercise is a must. A horse who is worked hard every day will be relaxed and, possibly more important, tired. His mind can be occupied by the anticipation of play and exercise beforehand and rest afterwards.

A few horses, particularly young ones, seem to need some preoccupation in the stall in addition to exercise. Such "toys" as a tether ball secured to a stall wall will amuse a restless animal. When installing any plaything, however, the tiniest detail of safety must be considered. Can he get a foot through it or caught in it? What would happen if he bit it? Can it lodge somewhere and become dangerous for him to retrieve it? Horses are alert and intelligent enough to need to stay busy, but they are seldom aware of hidden dangers, especially in their domicile.

If, in spite of all efforts to prevent it, an owner suspects his horse of pursuing an unpleasant activity, he or she should take immediate action to find out what it is and why. A close observation of the horse in his stall might reveal the needed answers. Has there been any change in routine or neighbors? Is he getting enough to eat? Is he uncomfortable (heat, cold, flies, illness, etc.)? Is he lonely? Does he resent the presence of people or other horses, or does he crave it?

If he is an impatient animal, it would be wise to feed him first. He can be munching happily instead of pawing or banging while everyone else gets fed. The telltale sounds of grain scoops and hay rustling can electrify some horses. If he resents his neighbors, they should be eliminated from his view. On the other hand, if he wants company, provisions should be made for seeing and possibly visiting the others.

A thorough check by a veterinarian is high on the priority list. Sometimes minor but irritating discomforts cause unsettling restlessness but can be easily remedied. If he's just downright lonesome, perhaps an inexpensive radio played constantly in the barn would soothe him. A station with an equal amount of music and human voices would make him feel someone is nearby. A variety of stable mates are in use throughout the horse world. Chickens, cats, dogs or goats appear frequently as equine comrades. There are recurring stories of horses who won't eat or play unless their favorite barn buddy is around.

When the vice cannot be suppressed, the burden of safety is then shifted to the habit itself. The horse must be protected from damage while he is performing it. Following are several common vices which seem most prone to enslave horses.

## Shying

This startling occurrence has dumped more riders than all deliberate bucks and pitches combined. The horse is primarily a fearful creature who is physically designed for quick responses and a rapid getaway. A rider is tinkering with the most basic instinct when he or she attempts to eradicate shying. It is the way a horse handles his spookiness that makes him dangerous or predictable.

Some mounts will suspiciously eye a frightening object, arch their necks, give it a wide berth and go right on. Others might catch a brief glimpse of it and hit the lift-off button. There are some horses who could saunter past an erupting volcano. But he has brothers and sisters somewhere who come unglued if a dry leaf drifts down within sight.

Horses who habitually shy can be victims of boredom and lack of exercise. Their surplus energy finds an awkward outlet in being jumpy. These animals usually look for extra monsters in addition to spooking at the ones which really exist. Such ''booger hunters'' usually reform with a lot of riding and hard work.

There are horses who possess a timid nature. They react to strange objects and sudden movements out of genuine fear. A confident, patient handler is the only cure for his insecurities. When a rider feels the horse tense up and collect himself for a six-foot lateral, he or she should not panic. A rapid shortening of the reins, a quick grab for the saddle horn and increased grip with the legs simply tells the horse ''You're right, it's dangerous; I'm scared, too.''

While a rider must prepare for any sudden movement, it can be done coolly. Slowly gathering the reins and speaking to the animal in calm tones will do much to convince him it's not as bad as he thinks it is. Another reassuring courtesy of the rider would be to allow the horse a little time to look the horror over. If he can assure himself it's not going to get him and eat him, he might be braver next time.

A fear of water is not uncommon among horses. A few will never get over it. Often, following other horses through a stream or being herded through water in the midst of a mass of horseflesh will do the trick. Some horses would never cross a creek if every other horse in the world was on the other side. But moving water is not always the culprit. Numerous horses would try to climb a tree before they would step into a puddle.

Water shyness usually has such a hold on a horse, it is a baffling problem. Any logical — not cruel or extreme — idea should be tried. Perhaps situating an above-ground feeding area outside and in the middle of a large puddle would help. The lure of fresh hay and sweet grain might entice him into the water where he'll have to stand while he eats. This won't guarantee, however, he'll voluntarily enter water at any other time.

Then there is the sneaky horse who shies because it is the fastest way to unload and head for home. A cunning horse will rapidly develop a habit of shying with certain riders he knows will give up easily. Some of these same mounts are pictures of courage with a firm-handed, experienced rider in the saddle. Others will try the jump-and-run trick with everybody who climbs aboard.

The best correction for this is a rider who can stay on and administer quick, immediate, reasonable punishment, such as a swift whack with a crop. The owner must be certain the horse is play-acting, though. Punishment for real fear does more harm than good. The pretender will give himself away if he shies at things away from the barn that he will accept or ignore around it. And too, if all the ogres are after him when he is going out and not along the same route coming back, he has let his secret slip.


## Cribbing

This is probably the most distressing and misunderstood vice of all. It is also one of the most detrimental to the horse. If Ol' Termite is chewing the barn down, he needs help.

The common misconception is that a cribber enjoys eating wood. While he may chew on a wooden surface, it is not for the purpose of consuming it. He firmly grips a wooden edge with his teeth and gulps air. The offender is this passage of air into the stomach. Horses have been known to die exhibiting the symptoms of colic, when an overload of air was the cause of death.

No one has advanced an irrefutable theory as to why horses crib. An obvious explanation would be to fill an empty or uncomfortable stomach with something. But this is disproved when a wormed, well-fed, otherwise healthy horse will abandon the contents of a feed box for the box, itself. It is a fact that severe cribbers are undernourished. They would rather practice their freakish intake of air than eat.

The use of plastic feed buckets and the removal of as many inviting edges as possible will cut down on the problem. There are hot, vile-tasting washes to be painted on areas such as window sills, door sills and beams. Sometimes it will repel, sometimes not. Several strap and shield contraptions have been devised to prevent the horse from getting a firm hold on the wood or to make it difficult to open his throat and swallow air. In some cases, turning a horse out to pasture will stop his cribbing. While this is probably the most widely successful solution, a horse with a tendency to crib should be watched. A few dedicated cribbers will set their teeth in a stump or wooden fence post and keep at it.

### Kicking

A kicker may be nervous, ill-tempered or pushy. Foals kick up blindly when playing, but when a horse takes aim, it's time to take action. Until this dangerous habit is broken, he should be kept a safe distance from other horses and people.

Horses lose interest in kicking when the offending foot is promptly tied up for thirty minutes or so. Such a training method takes long-term, steady monitoring of the horse, but it might discourage an automatic use of his feet. Another device with a definite message is a leather strap with a chain dangling from it. Fasten the leather strap around the horse's leg just above the hock. Any kicking action will deliver a smart rap by the chain on the horse's sensitive leg bones.

### Rearing

If a horse rears while being ridden, the safest measure is some sort of tie-down. A horse must be able to settle back on his hindquarters and thrust his head upward in order to lift his foreparts off the ground. If he can't get his head high enough, he can't distribute his weight to stand up.

A horse who rears in the stall also needs special precautions. There should be no projecting beams. There should be no slats, openings, mangers or ledges he could accidentally come down on or get hung over. If every possible snag is not removed, he should be stabled without a halter. Ideally, the ceiling should be much too high for him to reach. If not, it should be padded. Soft objects suspended from the ceiling just above the horse's head might make rearing less appealing. Here again, plenty of exercise will help keep a rearing horse earthbound.

### Weaving

Constant swaying back and forth in a stall is a sure sign of boredom. Too many hours standing in a cell necessitates some kind of physical action. Weaving is a relatively innocent vice, but its implication is sad. A restless, discontent animal is a miserable one. The owner should watch for stall damage if the horse rocks in one place. If a hole is dug in an earthen floor, a potential foot-trapping leg breaker is created between the ground and the wall's bottom edge. A few hours a day in an arena, pasture or a safe barn hall will take the edge off a weaver.

## Pacing

Walking to and fro in a stall is another manifestation of unbearable restlessness. The only difference between pacing and weaving is the the pacer will damage his floor more rapidly and more severely. Frequent romps in the wide open spaces are usually the only cure.


## Tail rubbing

The first step when a horse begins to rub his tail is with a veterinarian. Internal or external parasites are possible causes. The doctor can also detect any causative skin irritation.

If lice, worms or eczema are not found, look elsewhere. Any wounds or raw spots should be constantly doctored. It would help to tie him securely away from a wall or post, particularly if the owner could catch the horse in action and immediately stop it. Chronic tail rubbers might give it up after spending several days or weeks in a tie stall.


## Knee Banging

Knee banging is a classic attention-getter. This trick is performed at the stall door, window or in a trailer. If a horse does it only at feeding time or when some activity is going on, preferential treatment is in order. Feed him first, load him first, or work him first. When he's not acutely aware of the attention other animals are getting, he'll stop. Banging in the trailer will often subside when he is fed as soon as he is loaded.

If catering to his desire to be first doesn't work, pad his favorite area. The lack of noise makes banging a lot less fun. Certainly, it decreases the risk of injury, though most horses won't bang hard enough to damage themselves. And too, the chain used on a kicking horse will do the same thing when attached to a front leg.

No horse is perfect, yet those who acquire serious vices remain in the minority. Horse owners must remember that each animal is as individual as a person. One horse's reaction to a situation will be unlike any other's. His habits are all his own. How each responds to a person's effort to change him will be strictly unique. In coping with bad habits as in every other facet of caring for a horse, patience, understanding, logic and consistency are the only successful attitudes.

# Appendix I

## Parts of the Horse

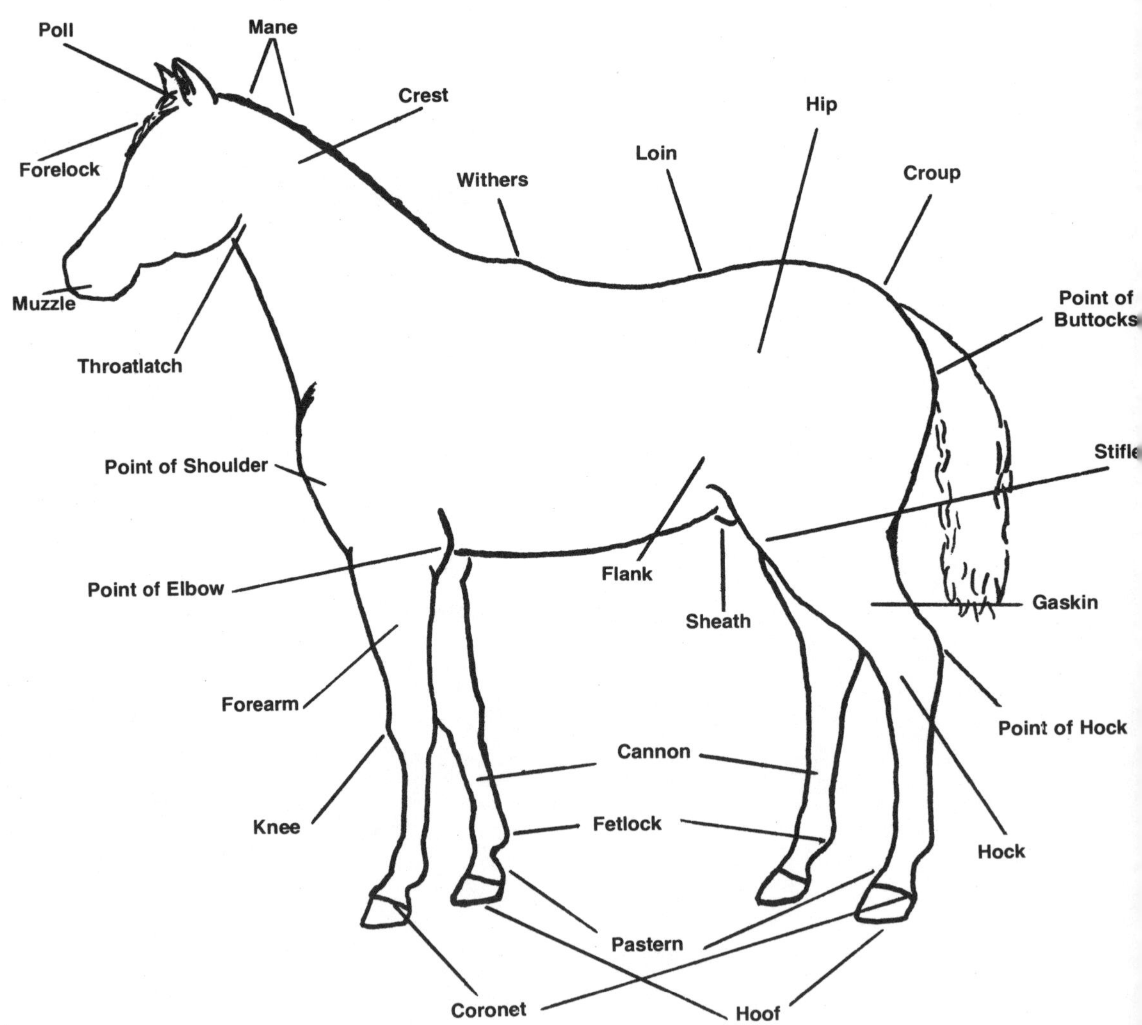

## Common Leg and Face Markings

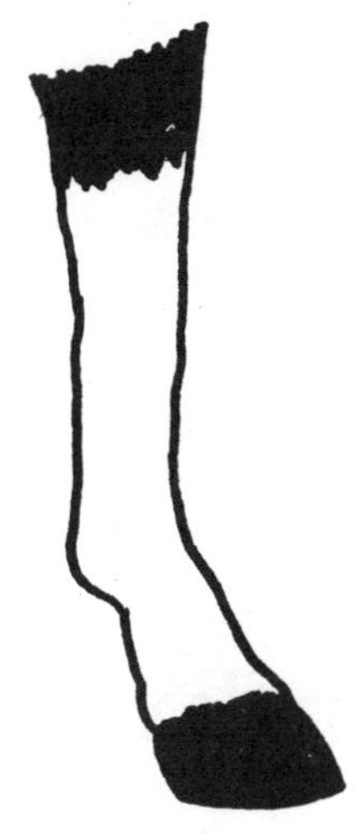

**Stocking**

**Half Stocking**

**Pastern**

**Coronet**

## Common Leg Markings

**Snip**

**Stripe**

**Star**

**Blaze**

**Bald Face**

## Common Face Markings

# Appendix II

## Breed Associations and Registries

All Breeds Horse Registry, The
Box 401
Sheridan, Wyoming 82801

American Albino Association, Inc.
Box 79
Crabtree, Oregon 97335

American Andalusian Horse Association
Box 1290
Silver City, New Mexico 88061

American Association of Owners and Breeders of Peruvian Paso Horses
Box 282
Santa Ynez, California 93460

American Bashkir Curly Registry
Box 453
Ely, Nevada 89301

American Buckskin Registry Association
Box 1125
Anderson, California 96007

American Connemara Pony Society
c/o R. D. 2, Featherbed Lane
Ballston Spa, New York 12020

American Donkey and Mule Society
2410 Executive Drive
Indianapolis, Indiana 46261

American Fox Trotting Horse Breed Association, Inc.
100½ S. Crittenden
Marshfield, Missouri 65706

American Gotland Horse Association
R. R. 2, Box 181
Elkland, Missouri 65644

American Hackney Horse Society
Peekskill Towers
Lakeside Drive
Peekskill, New York 10566

American Indian Horse Registry
P. O. Box 9192
Phoenix, Arizona 85020

American Morgan Horse Association, Inc.
Box 9, W. Lake Moraine Road
Hamilton, New York 13346

American Mustang Association
Box 122
Berlin, Wisconsin 54923

American Paint Horse Association
P. O. Box 12487
Fort Worth, Texas 76116

American Part-blooded Horse Registry
4120 S. E. River Drive
Portland, Oregon 97222

American Paso Fino Horse Association, Inc.
Mellon Bank Building, Room 3018
525 William Penn Place
Pittsburgh, Pennsylvania 15219

American Quarter Horse Association
2736 West Tenth Street
Amarillo, Texas 79105

American Quarter Pony Association
c/o Harold Wymore
New Sharon, Iowa 50207

American Saddlebred Pleasure Horse Association
801 South Court Street
Scott City, Kansas 67871

American Saddle Horse Breeders Association
929 South Fourth Street
Louisville, Kentucky 40203

American Shetland Pony Club
Box 468
Fowler, Indiana 47944

American Shire Horse Association
6960 Northwest Drive
Ferndale, Washington 98248

American Suffolk Horse Association
672 Polk Boulevard
Des Moines, Iowa 50312

American Walking Horse Association
753 Herkimer Road
Utica, New York 13502

American Walking Pony Association
Route 5, Box 88
Upper River Road
Macon, Georgia 31201

Appaloosa Horse Club
Box 8403
Moscow, Idaho 83843

Appaloosa Horse Club of Canada
Box 3036, Postal Station "B"
Calgary, Alberta, Canada

Arabian Horse Registry of America
7801 E. Belleview Avenue
Englewood, Colorado 80110

Arabian Horse Society, The
Box 85
Lebanon, Ohio 45036

Belgian Draft Horse Corporation of American
282 South Wabash Street
Box 335
Wabash, Indiana 46992

Chickasaw Horse Association
Love Valley, North Carolina 28677

Cleveland Bay Society of America
c/o Lucky Hit Farm
White Post, Virginia 22663

Clydesdale Breeders of the United States
Rt. 3
Waverly, Iowa 50677

Colorado Ranger Horse Association, Inc.
7023 Eden Mill Road
Woodbine, Maryland 21797

Galiceno Horse Breeders Association, Inc.
111 E. Elm Street
Tyler, Texas 75701

Half-Arab and Anglo-Arab Registries
224 East Olive Avenue
Burbank, California 91503

Half-bred Stud Book and Half-Thoroughbred Registry
c/o American Remount Association
Box 1066
Perris, California 92370

Half-Saddlebred Registry of America
600 Poplar Street
Cashecton, Ohio 43812

International Arabian Horse Association
224 East Olive Avenue
Burbank, California 91503

International Buckskin Horse Association, Inc.
Box 357
St. John, Indiana 46373

Mid-America Fox Trotting Horse Association
3440 E. Sunshine
Springfield, Missouri 65804

Missouri Fox Trotting Horse Association
Box 637
Ava, Missouri 65608

Morab Horse Registry of America
Box 143
Clovis, California 93612

Morgan Horse Club
10 Crossroads Plaza
West Hartford, Connecticut 06117

Morocco Spotted Horse Association of America
R. R. 1
Ridott, Illinois 61067

National Appaloosa Pony, Inc.
112½ East Eighth
Rochester, Indiana 46975

National Chickasaw Horse Association
c/o Rt. 2
Clarinda, Iowa 51632

National Mustang Association
Newcastle, Utah 84756

National Palomino Breeders Association
c/o East Dixie Street
London, Kentucky 40741

National Quarter Horse Registry
Raywood, Texas 77582

National Trotting Pony Association, Inc.
575 Broadway
Hanover, Pennsylvania 17331

Original Half Quarter Horse Registry
Hubbard, Oregon 97032

Palomino Horse Association
Box 324
Jefferson City, Missouri 65101

Palomino Horse Breeders of America
Box 249
Mineral Wells, Texas 76067

Paso Fino Owners and Breeders Association, Inc.
Box 2725
Valdosta, Georgia 31601

Percheron Horse Association of America
Route 1
Belmont, Ohio 43718

Peruvian Paso Horse Registry of North America
Box 816
Guerneville, California 95446

Pinto Horse Association of America
Box 3984
San Diego, California 92103

Pony of the Americas Club
Box 1447
Mason City, Iowa 50401

Racking Horse Breeders' Association of America
Headquarters: Birmingham, Alabama
Mailing Address: Helena, Alabama 35080

Spanish-Barb Breeders Association
Box 7479
Colorado Springs, Colorado 80907

Spanish Mustang Registry
Route 2, Box 74
Marshall, Texas 75670

Standardbred Owners Association
539 Old Country Road
Westbury, New York 11590

Standard Quarter Horse Association
4390 Fenton Street
Denver, Colorado 80212

Tennessee Walking Horse Breeders' Association of America
250 N. Ellington Parkway
Lewisburg, Tennessee 37091

United States Trotting Association
  (Standardbreds)
750 Michigan Avenue
Columbus, Ohio 43215

U. S. Trotting Pony Association
Box 468
Fowler, Indiana 47944

Welsh Pony Society of America
c/o L. F. Gehret
Glenmoore, Pennsylvania 19343

# Appendix III

## Addresses of Special Interest

Handicapped

North American Riding for the
Handicapped Association
R. D. 1, Box 22
Sewickly, Pennsylvania 15143

Health and Animal Protection Agencies

Alberta Department of Agriculture
Horse Industry Branch
8th floor, Agriculture Building
9718 107th Street
Edmonton, Alberta
Canada T5K 2C8

American Association of Equine
Practitioners
Route 5, 14 Hillcrest Circle
Golden, Colorado 80401

American Horse Council
1776 K Street, N. W.
Washington, D. C. 20006

American Horse Protection Association
629 Rover Bend Road
Great Falls, Virginia 22066

American Humane Association
Box 1266
Denver, Colorado 80201

American Society for the Prevention of Cruelty to Animals
441 East 92nd Street
New York, New York 10028

American Veterinary Medical Association
600 S. Michigan Avenue
Chicago, Illinois 60605

Committee for Humane Legislation
11 West 60th Street
New York, New York 10023

Humane Society of the United States
1604 K Street, N. W.
Washington, D. C. 20006

International Society for the Protection of Mustangs and Burros
c/o 140 Greenstone Drive
Reno, Nevada 89502

Morris Animal Foundation
531 Guaranty Bank Building
Denver, Colorado 80202

Society for Animal Protective
  Legislation
Box 3719
Georgetown Station
Washington, D. C. 20007

United States Animal Health Association
1444 E. Main Street
Richmond, Virginia 23219

Wild Horse Organized Assistance
Box 555
Reno, Nevada 89504

Women's Veterinary Medical As-
  sociation
c/o Dr. Bonnie V. Gustafson
College of Veterinary Medicine
Texas A. & M.
College Station, Texas 77843

Horse Racing

American Trainers Association
P. O. Box 6702
Towson, Maryland 21204

Arabian Horse Racing Association
  of America
66 S. Riverside Drive
Batavia, Ohio 45103

Harness Horsemen International
Passante Professional Center
61 Cook Hill Road
Windsor, Connecticut 06095

Jockey Club, The
300 Park Avenue
New York, New York 10022

Thoroughbred Owners and Breed-
  ers Association
Box 4038
Lexington, Kentucky 40504

Thoroughbred Racing Associations
5 Dakota Drive
Lake Success
Hyde Park, New York 12538

Rodeo and Cowboy Associations

American Black Cowboy Association
455 Elizabeth Avenue Suite 14-A
Newark, New Jersey 07112

Girl's Rodeo Association
Box 86
Addington, Oklahoma 73520

International Rodeo Association
American Fidelity Building, Suites
  412-418
Box 615
Pauls Valley, Oklahoma 73075

International Rodeo Association,
  Humane Activities Office
Box 8160
Nashville, Tennessee 37207

National Cowboy Hall of Fame
  and Western Heritage Center
1700 Northeast 63rd Street
Oklahoma City, Oklahoma 73111

National High School Rodeo As-
  sociation
Rt. 4, Box 87
Rapid City, South Dakota 57701

National Intercollegiate Rodeo
  Association
Box 2088 S.H.S.U.
Huntsville, Texas 77340

National Little Britches Rodeo
  Association
Box 651
Littleton, Colorado 80120

Rodeo Cowboys Association
2929 West 19th Avenue
Denver, Colorado 80204

Rodeo Information Foundation
2929 West 19th Avenue
Denver, Colorado 80204

Southwestern Pioneer Cowboys
  Association
Box 82
Benson, Arizona 85602

Special Interest

American Horse Publications
5314 Bingle Road
Houston, Texas 77018

American Horse Shows Association
527 Madison Avenue.
New York, New York 10022

Carriage Association of America, The
c/o 885 Forest Avenue
Portland, Maine 04103

Horsemen's United Association
Lamb's Bridge
South Fork, Pennsylvania 15956

International Union of Journeymen Horseshoers of the United States and Canada
8795 S. W. 99th Street
Miami, Florida 33143

National Cutting Horse Association
Box 12155
Fort Worth, Texas 76116

National Reining Horse Association
c/o Garvey
R. R. 2
Greenville, Ohio 45331

Professional Horsemen's Association of America
R. D. 1, Box 22
Sewickly, Pennsylvania 15143

Shetland Pony Identification Bureau
1108 Jackson Street
Omaha, Nebraska 68102

United States Equestrian Team, Inc.
Gladstone, New Jersey 07934

Walking Horse Trainers Association
Box 61
Shelbyville, Tennessee 37160

Western Apparel and Equipment Manufacturers Association
Box 4044, Station A
Albuquerque, New Mexico 87106

Western History Association
University of Oklahoma
Norman, Oklahoma 73069

Trail and Wilderness Riding

American Association of Sheriff Posses and Riding Clubs
1318 W. Euless Boulevard
Euless, Texas 76039

High Sierra Packers' Association
Box 147
Bishop, California 93514

Indian Nations Trail Rides, Ltd.
625 South Monroe Street
Stillwater, Oklahoma 74074

International Trailriders Association, Inc.
419 N. Virginia
Roswell, New Mexico 88201

Montana Outfitters and Dude Ranchers Association
Box 382
Bozeman, Montana 59715

National Association of Trail Ride Competition
1995 Day Road
Gilroy, California 95020

Trail Riders of the Canadian Rockies
Box 6742
Postal Station D
Calgary, Alberta T2P 2E6
Canada

Trail Riders of the Wilderness
American Forestry Association
1319 18th Street, N. W.
Washington, D. C. 20036

Wilderness Society
729 15th Street, N. W.
Washington, D. C. 20005

# Glossary

ARENA  Large, fence enclosed area for working or performing.

BANDANA  Large, colored handkerchief used originally by range cowboys.

BARRIER  Gate or rope in front of a box or chute.

BARS  The toothless space between the incisors and molars in a horse's mouth where the bit rests. (The mouthpiece of a bit is often called the bar.)

BAT  Short, wide, flat leather riding whip.

BIT  Mouthpiece of a bridle.

BLANKET  (1) Heavy duck or canvas buckle-on covering for a horse. (2) Soft, heavy length of fabric used under a saddle to protect a horse's back. (3) The light, usually white, area over an Appaloosa's hindquarters containing darker spots.

BOSAL  Round, braided rawhide noseband.

BOX  Area beside a chute where ropers and steer wrestlers must stay until the exact moment for pursuit of calf or steer.

BRAND  (v.) Burning an owner's code or insignia into an animal's flesh with a heated iron.

BREAK  To introduce a horse to the saddle and gain his acceptance of a rider.

BREAST STRAP  Strap of leather connected to each front side of a saddle, passing under a horse's neck for the purpose of keeping the saddle from slipping backward out of place.

BREECHING  Strap of leather connected to each rear side of a saddle, passing under a horse's tail and resting well below it, for the purpose of keeping a pack or saddle from slipping forward out of place.

BRIDLE  Piece of equipment fitting a horse's head and holding a bit in his mouth with attached reins. It is for the purpose of controlling the horse from his back.

BRIDLE GAP   Area of roached mane just behind a horse's ears to allow free passage of the bridle's headstall.

BROKEN   (1) A horse's being trained to accept a rider. (2) When referring to a broken mouthpiece, it means a bit with a moveable joint in it.

BRONC   Bucking horse.

BUCK   Act of a horse's lowering his head and snapping his body in the middle, lifting all four feet off the ground at once.

CANTER   Slow, animated gallop characterized by higher action in the foreparts than in the rear.

CANTLE   Rear part of a saddle; usually refers to the raised, curving back portion of its seat.

CHAPS   Leather zip- or snap-on leggings.

CHUTE   Narrow enclosure for containing horses or cattle.

CINCH   (v.) To tighten the girth on a saddle or pack; (n.) *see* GIRTH.

COLIC   Painful abdominal upset.

COLLECT   A horse's preparing himself for action. He will tense, pull in his chin, move his hind legs up under him.

COLT   Young male horse.

CONFORMATION   Build, shape, proportionment.

COW KICK   Act of a horse's kicking out a hind leg to the side rather than straight back.

CRIBBING   Act of a horse's setting his teeth on a wooden object and sucking in air.

CRICKET   Roller in the port of a bit.

CROP   (1) Small, flexible but rigid riding whip ending in a loop. (2. v.) To trim or cut off.

CROSS-FIRE   Activity in which a horse's rear foot strikes the back of his diagonally opposite front foot when in motion.

CURB BIT   Any bridle's mouthpiece whose action is produced on the principle of a lever rather than direct pulling.

CURB CHAIN   Short length of chain, preferably flat-sided, attached to the bit, resting behind the horse's chin for the purpose of intensifying the bit's action in the mouth.

CURB STRAP   Short length of leather attached to the bit, resting behind the horse's chin for the purpose of intensifying the bit's action in the mouth.

CUT   Act of selecting a cow, calf, steer or bull in a herd, removing it from the herd and keeping it separated from it.

DALLY   A single turn of a rope around the saddle horn.

DEADHEAD   (1) Slang for a lifeless, slow-moving animal. (2) Slang for a horse and rider running hard and fast, as in a race.

EQUESTRIAN   Accomplished horse rider.

EQUINE   Name encompassing all members of the horse family.

EQUITATION   Proper, accomplished, correct horse riding.

FARRIER   Professional horseshoer.

FILLY   Young female horse.

FLEXION   The dropping and tucking inward of a horse's head; his manner of bending his neck.

FOAL   (v.) Act of a mare's presenting a newborn horse. (2) A newborn or extremely young horse.

FORGING   Act of a horse's hitting his forefoot with the hind foot on the same side when he is in motion. The front of the back hoof usually strikes the inside of the front toe as it is being lifted off the ground. Often, the rear foot will strike the back point of his front shoe.

FORK   Front, open part of a saddle or saddle tree which rests over a horse's withers.

GAIT   Any one of a horse's natural ways of going: walk, a four-beat slow, easy movement; trot or jog, a two-beat, slightly faster movement in which a horse's two diagonal feet strike the ground together; lope, a faster, three-beat movement with hind legs driving and front legs lifting and reaching.

GALLOP   The fastest natural gait, slightly faster than a lope, slightly slower than a run.

GEAR   Horse, trail, camping, ranch or show equipment.

GELDING   A castrated horse.

GIRTH   Belly band used to secure a pack or saddle to a horse's back.

GREEN   Inexperienced; just beginning training.

GYMKHANA   Series of athletic contests, especially races.

HACKAMORE   Type of bridle which employs nose and lower jaw pressure for control rather than metal in the mouth.

HALTER   Rope, leather or nylon equipment fitting the horse's head, used for leading or tying.

HAND   Unit of measure for gauging a horse's height. One hand is four inches.

HAZER   Mounted assistant in some rodeo team events, particularly steer wrestling.

HEADER   Member of a roping team who is responsible for roping a calf's or steer's head.

HEART   Courage, will, ambition, dedication.

HEAT   (1) Mare's fertile period. (2) Each segment of a race or game containing different participants.

HONDA   Small loop through which the rope passes to form a lariat.

HORSEMANSHIP   General knowledge of horses combined with proficiency at handling them.

INSTINCT   Inborn pattern of responses.

JOG   A slow, smooth, level-backed trot; a jogging horse takes shorter, less animated steps than does a trotting horse.

JUDGE   (n.) Official of a horse show who determines winners in the classes. (v). To officiate in a horse show by selecting the winning horses.

JUNIOR HORSES   Class designation in horse shows for horses four years of age and younger.

LARIAT   The loop formed in a rope to catch an animal.

LEAD   (1, n.) The forefoot which has impact with the ground initially and independently of the other feet. The leading rear foot must correspond. A horse should lead with the foot which is on the inside of a turn. Example: If a horse is traveling in a right-turning direction, he should be on the right lead. (2, v.) Act of directing a horse in motion from the ground by a rope or lead shank secured to his head area or a halter.

LEAD SHANK   Length of rope or leather connected to a halter to lead a horse.

LOGGING   Dragging a log or other heavy object behind a horse from the saddle.

LONGE   To work a horse on a rope in a circle around the handler.

LONGE LINE   Rope used for longeing a horse.

MOUNT   (n.) A saddle horse. (v.) To get up on a horse.

MUZZLE   Horse's nose, mouth and chin area.

NECK REIN   Turning and maneuvering a horse by laying the reins on one side of the horse's neck or the other.

NICKER   Quiet, low murmur of a horse.

OVERO   Color designation of Pinto horses in which the coat is a solid color with irregular patches of white along the midsections of the neck, sides and flanks.

PACING   (1) Habit of a horse in which he walks back and forth constantly. (2) Horse gait in which both legs on the same side of his body move simultaneously.

PARASITE   Organisms living in the skin or entrails of an animal.

PATTERN   (1) Order in which various skills are executed in a horse show class. Patterns often involve obstacles or standards. (2) Appearance of color in a horse's coat.

PICKUP MEN   Mounted riders in a rodeo arena who take cowboys off bucking broncs after a ride.

PIGGING STRING   Short length of rope used to tie a calf's or steer's legs after it has been roped.

PIVOT   Maneuver in which a horse collects his weight on his haunches and performs a complete or near complete turn. His hind feet remain in place, and he does not touch the ground with either forefoot between the start and finish of a turn.

POMMEL   High, front portion of a saddle.

PONCHO   Cape-styled garment with a hood and coming to the wearer's feet (usually rain-repellent).

PONY   (v.) To lead a young horse in training from an older, experienced horse.

PORT   Curve in the center of a bit's mouthpiece.

POST   (v.) Alternately standing and sitting every other beat of a trot. (Most Western riders do not post, they sit the jog trot.)

POT   Combination of all entry fees in an event.

PUREBRED   Animal whose ancestors are all of the same breed.

QUARTER HORSE   A stocky, heavily muscled horse, bred for maneuverability, steady disposition, and cow sense. The breed name originated from the quarter-mile races developed to exhibit the horses' matchless speed in short distances. (See Chapter One)

QUIRT   Small riding whip with a short handle and a length of braided leather.

RATING   Act of a pursuing horse staying in the proper position relative to a calf or steer to allow his rider to rope or wrestle the animal.

REAR   (v.) Act of a horse's settling back on his hind legs and lifting his foreparts off the ground until he is virtually standing up.

RESIN   Extremely sticky substance obtained from plants, usually pine trees.

RIGGING   Equipment; saddles and their features.

RING   A work or performance area, usually bounded by a fence and shaped in a long oval.

RING STEWARD   Horse-show official who keeps order and gives contestants directions in the ring. Most judges do not approach entrants personally, but indicate to a ring steward (sometimes called a ring master) what is to be done.

ROACHED   Mane trimmed short, completely to the neck.

ROLLBACK   Maneuver in which a galloping horse stops, lifts his foreparts, swings around to a complete reverse and starts out again at a gallop on the correct lead.

ROMEL   End connector of closed, braided rawhide reins.

ROWEL   Rotating wheel constructed with points, either sharp or dull, at the back of a spur.

RUN-OFF   Repeat of a race between tying contestants for the purpose of breaking the tie.

SANCTION   Recognition of a horse show by a particular breed registry or association for the accumulation of points by its entrants.

SCORING   (1) In roping or steer wrestling events, getting to the calf or steer as soon as possible after it is out of its chute; allowing a calf or steer to cross the scoring line before the roper or wrestler may leave the box. (2) Completing a performance satisfactorily enough to receive a score by the judge or judges.

SCORING LINE   Designated distance in front of a calf's or steer's chute which he must cross before the roper or wrestler is allowed out of the box.

SCOTCH   (1) Brace to prevent slipping. (2) Fault developed by a mishandled roping horse; anticipating a painful jerk on his mouth, he'll tuck his chin and start stopping prematurely.

SEAT   Position of a mounted rider in the saddle.

SENIOR HORSES   Class designation in horse shows for horses five years of age and older.

SERPENTINE   (v.) Weave in and out around obstacles in a certain line of direction.

SHANK   Portion of the bit from the mouthpiece to the reins.

SHY   (adj.) Fearful. (v.) To panic, bolt and run at an unfamiliar object, noise, etc.

SLICKER   Wide-bottomed raincoat designed to fit over a mounted rider and the saddle.

SNAFFLE   Bit with a center jointed mouthpiece.

SNUBBING POST   Post used to secure a roped animal.

SPADE BIT   Extremely severe Spanish bit, consisting of a high spade-shaped port, cricket and often chains.

SPOOKY   Easily frightened.

STANDARD   A pole, barrel, log or other object used in a horse show class to designate a pattern or serve as a marker.

STEER   Castrated male bovine.

STOCK   (1) Cattle, horses, other livestock. (2) A *stock* horse is one which is used for working with livestock.

TACK   Horse equipment, principally saddles and bridles.

TIE-DOWN   Strap connected to a bridle's nosepiece and to the saddle's girth to prevent a horse's raising his head to excess.

TOBIANO   Color designation of Pinto horses in which the coat is white with large, smooth areas of color on the head, upper neck, chest, flanks and tail.

TRACTABLE   Easily managed.

TREE   Foundation upon which a saddle is constructed.

TROT   *See* GAIT.

USING HORSE   Horse that regularly performs various working chores as opposed to a show horse.

VAQUERO   Mexican cowboy.

VICE   Bad, sometimes dangerous habit.

WALK   *See* GAIT.

WEANLING   Animal just removed from his mother's side.

WEAVING   A horse's standing in one place and swaying back and forth.

WHINNY   The call of a horse.

WITHERS   The uppermost point of a horse's shoulders.

WORKING THE ROPE   Activity in which a horse faces a roped calf and maintains proper pull and direction on the rope.

WORKOUT   Work or performance activity.

WORMING   Act of inducing a parasite-killing substance into an animal's stomach

WRANGLING   Tending to horses or horse herds.

YEARLING   Animal which has attained or just passed one year of age.

# Index